HERSHEY'S®
Bake Shoppe ™
COOKIES

Publications International, Ltd.

All recipes developed and tested by the Hershey Kitchens.

Photography: Proffitt Photography, Chicago
Photographers: Laurie Proffitt, Cindy Trim
Prop Stylist: Kathy Lapin
Food Stylists: Carol Smoler, Mary Helen Steindler, Josephine Orba
Assistant Food Stylist: Lee Mooney
Photographer's Assistant: Russell Bailey

Pictured on the front cover *(clockwise from top right):* Walnut MiniChip Biscotti *(page 86),* Almond Shortbread Cookies with Raspberry Filling *(page 81),* Hershey's Classic Chocolate Chip Cookies *(page 29)* and Ultimate Chocolate Brownies *(page 10).*

Pictured on the back cover *(clockwise from top right):* Chocolate Chip 'n Oatmeal Cookies *(page 24),* P.B. Chips Brownie Cups *(page 36)* and Chocolate Chips and Raspberry Bars *(page 88).*

ISBN: 0-7853-2094-6

Manufactured in U.S.A.

8 7 6 5 4 3 2 1

Nutritional Analysis: Nutritional information is given for some of the recipes in this publication. Each analysis is based on the food items in the ingredient list. When more than one ingredient choice is listed, the first ingredient is used for analysis.

Microwave Cooking: Microwave ovens vary in wattage. The microwave cooking times given in this publication are approximate. Use the cooking times as guidelines and check for doneness before adding more time. Consult manufacturer's instructions for suitable microwave-safe cooking dishes.

MIX IT UP WITH HERSHEY'S!   4

CHOCOLATETOWN CLASSICS   6

KIDS' KITCHEN   30

TREATS WITH A TWIST   50

COMPANY'S COMING   74

RECIPE INDEX   92

PRODUCT INDEX   94

MIX IT UP WITH HERSHEY'S!

There's nothing like a batch of freshly baked cookies, hot from the oven. The aroma fills the house and before you know it, the whole family is in the kitchen waiting to enjoy warm cookies and ice cold milk.

Hershey's Bake Shoppe Cookies cookbook is devoted to cookies, cookies and more cookies! The recipes featured are representative of the wonderful treats you can make with the extensive line of *Hershey's Bake Shoppe* pieces that include:

Hershey's Semi-Sweet Chocolate Chips—Classic, deep, rich, semi-sweet chocolate.

Hershey's MiniChips Chocolate—A slightly smaller version of *Hershey's* Semi-Sweet Chocolate Chips with the same great taste. Ideal for muffins, cakes and pies.

Hershey's Milk Chocolate Chips—Creamy *Hershey's* milk chocolate.

Hershey's Premier White Chips—Delicious vanilla taste.

Hershey's Butterscotch Chips—Rich butterscotch flavor.

Hershey's Raspberry Chips—If you love chocolate and raspberry, you'll love these raspberry-flavored semi-sweet chocolate chips.

Hershey's Mint Chocolate Chips—Semi-sweet chocolate chips with refreshing mint flavor.

Hershey's Reduced Fat Baking Chips—Half the available fat of the traditional semi-sweet chips.

Hershey's Mini Kisses Chocolate—*Hershey's Kisses* Chocolates, but ⅓ the size. Unwrapped and ready to be poured into batter.

Skor English Toffee Bits—The toffee center of a *Skor* candy bar broken into pieces perfect for baking and toppings.

Almond Joy Coconut and Almond Bits—Bits of almond surrounded by coconut and milk chocolate.

Hershey's Holiday Bits—Semi-sweet chocolate surrounded by bright red, white and green candy coatings.

Reese's Peanut Butter Chips—*Reese's* peanut butter taste in a chip.

Reese's Peanut Butter Bits—Peanut butter surrounded by milk chocolate and candy coating.

And of course, there's *Hershey's* Cocoa, *Hershey's* Baking Chocolate, *Mounds* Coconut and *Reese's* Peanut Butter.

With such a variety of products to choose from, the possibilities are endless! We've included an index by recipe and product to make it easy for you to find the perfect cookie recipe. Have fun making exciting, new cookies each time you bake! Enjoy!

CHOCOLATETOWN CLASSICS

HERSHEY'S "PERFECTLY CHOCOLATE" CHOCOLATE CHIP COOKIES

2¼ cups all-purpose flour
⅓ cup HERSHEY'S Cocoa
1 teaspoon baking soda
½ teaspoon salt
1 cup (2 sticks) butter or margarine, softened
¾ cup granulated sugar
¾ cup packed light brown sugar

1 teaspoon vanilla extract
2 eggs
2 cups (12-ounce package) HERSHEY'S Semi-Sweet Chocolate Chips
1 cup chopped nuts (optional)

1. Heat oven to 375°F.

2. Stir together flour, cocoa, baking soda and salt. In large bowl, beat butter, granulated sugar, brown sugar and vanilla on medium speed of electric mixer until creamy. Add eggs; beat well. Gradually add flour mixture, beating until well blended. Stir in chocolate chips and nuts, if desired. Drop by rounded teaspoons onto ungreased cookie sheet.

3. Bake 8 to 10 minutes or until set. Cool slightly; remove from cookie sheet to wire rack.   *About 5 dozen cookies*

Hershey's "Perfectly Chocolate" Chocolate Chip Cookies

BROWNIE CARAMEL PECAN BARS

½ cup sugar
2 tablespoons butter or
 margarine
2 tablespoons water
2 cups (12-ounce
 package) HERSHEY'S
 Semi-Sweet Chocolate
 Chips, divided

2 eggs
1 teaspoon vanilla extract
⅔ cup all-purpose flour
¼ teaspoon baking soda
¼ teaspoon salt
 CARAMEL TOPPING
 (recipe follows)
1 cup pecan pieces

1. Heat oven to 350°F. Line 9-inch square baking pan with foil, extending foil over edges of pan. Grease and flour foil.

2. In medium saucepan, combine sugar, butter and water; cook over low heat, stirring constantly, until mixture boils. Remove from heat. Immediately add 1 cup chocolate chips; stir until melted. Beat in eggs and vanilla until well blended. Stir together flour, baking soda and salt; stir into chocolate mixture. Spread batter into prepared pan.

3. Bake 15 to 20 minutes or until brownies begin to pull away from sides of pan. Meanwhile, prepare CARAMEL TOPPING. Remove brownies from oven; immediately and carefully spread with prepared topping. Sprinkle remaining 1 cup chips and pecans over topping. Cool completely in pan on wire rack, being careful not to disturb chips while soft. Lift out of pan. Cut into bars.

About 16 bars

CARAMEL TOPPING: Remove wrappers from 25 caramels. In medium microwave-safe bowl, place ¼ cup (½ stick) butter or margarine, caramels and 2 tablespoons milk. Microwave at HIGH (100%) 1 minute; stir. Microwave an additional 1 to 2 minutes, stirring every 30 seconds, or until caramels are melted and mixture is smooth when stirred. Use immediately.

Brownie Caramel Pecan Bars

ULTIMATE CHOCOLATE BROWNIES

¾ cup HERSHEY'S Cocoa
½ teaspoon baking soda
⅔ cup butter or margarine,
    melted and divided
½ cup boiling water
2 cups sugar
2 eggs
1⅓ cups all-purpose flour

1 teaspoon vanilla extract
¼ teaspoon salt
1 cup HERSHEY'S Semi-
    Sweet Chocolate Chips
ONE–BOWL
    BUTTERCREAM
    FROSTING (recipe
    follows)

1. Heat oven to 350°F. Grease 13 × 9 × 2-inch baking pan or two 8-inch square baking pans.

2. In large bowl, stir together cocoa and baking soda; stir in ⅓ cup butter. Add boiling water; stir until mixture thickens. Stir in sugar, eggs and remaining ⅓ cup butter; stir until smooth. Add flour, vanilla and salt; blend completely. Stir in chocolate chips. Pour into prepared pan.

3. Bake 35 to 40 minutes for rectangular pan, 30 to 35 minutes for square pans or until brownies begin to pull away from sides of pan. Cool completely in pan on wire rack. Meanwhile, prepare ONE–BOWL BUTTERCREAM FROSTING; frost brownies. Cut into squares. *About 36 brownies*

ONE-BOWL BUTTERCREAM FROSTING

6 tablespoons butter or
    margarine, softened
2⅔ cups powdered sugar

½ cup HERSHEY'S Cocoa
⅓ cup milk
1 teaspoon vanilla extract

1. In medium bowl, beat butter. Add powdered sugar and cocoa alternately with milk; beat to spreading consistency (additional milk may be needed). Blend in vanilla. *About 2 cups frosting*

PEANUT BUTTER CHIP-GRANOLA BARS

¼ cup (½ stick) butter or margarine, softened
¼ cup shortening
1 cup packed light brown sugar
1 egg
1 teaspoon vanilla extract
1⅓ cups all-purpose flour
½ teaspoon baking soda
½ teaspoon ground cinnamon

½ teaspoon salt
¼ cup milk
1⅔ cups granola or natural cereal, crumbled
1 cup MOUNDS Sweetened Coconut Flakes
1 cup raisins
1⅔ cups (10-ounce package) REESE'S Peanut Butter Chips

1. Heat oven to 350°F. Line 15½ × 10½ × 1-inch jelly-roll pan with foil.

2. In large bowl, beat butter, shortening, brown sugar, egg and vanilla until well blended. Stir together flour, baking soda, cinnamon and salt; add alternately with milk to butter mixture, beating until well blended. Stir in granola, coconut, raisins and peanut butter chips. Spread batter into prepared pan.

3. Bake 20 to 25 minutes or until top is golden brown. Cool completely in pan on wire rack. Invert pan; peel off foil. Cut into bars.   *About 48 bars*

MINICHIP GRANOLA BARS: Substitute HERSHEY'S MINICHIPS Semi-Sweet Chocolate for peanut butter chips.

HERSHEY'S MILK CHOCOLATE CHIP GIANT COOKIES

6 tablespoons butter or margarine, softened
½ cup granulated sugar
¼ cup packed light brown sugar
½ teaspoon vanilla extract
1 egg

1 cup all-purpose flour
½ teaspoon baking soda
2 cups (11.5-ounce package) HERSHEY'S Milk Chocolate Chips
Frosting (optional)
Ice cream (optional)

1. Heat oven to 350°F. Line two 9-inch round baking pans with foil, extending foil over edge of pans.

2. Beat butter, granulated sugar, brown sugar and vanilla until light and fluffy. Add egg; beat well. Stir together flour and baking soda; gradually add to butter mixture, beating until well blended. Stir in milk chocolate chips. Spread one-half of batter into each prepared pan, spreading to 1 inch from edge. (Cookies will spread to edge when baking.)

3. Bake 15 to 20 minutes or until lightly browned. Cool completely; carefully lift cookies from pan and remove foil. Frost, if desired. Cut each cookie into wedges; serve topped with scoop of ice cream, if desired.   *About 12 to 16 servings*

 TIP

Bake cookies on the middle rack of the oven, one pan at a time. Uneven browning can occur if baking on more than one rack at the same time.

Hershey's Milk Chocolate Chip Giant Cookie

HERSHEY'S SOFT & CHEWY COOKIES

1 cup (2 sticks) butter (no substitutes)
¾ cup packed light brown sugar
½ cup granulated sugar
¼ cup light corn syrup
1 egg
2 teaspoons vanilla extract

2½ cups all-purpose flour
1 teaspoon baking soda
¼ teaspoon salt
1 package (10 to 12 ounces) HERSHEY'S Bake Shoppe pieces (any flavor)

1. Heat oven to 350°F.

2. In large bowl, beat butter, brown sugar and granulated sugar until light and fluffy. Add corn syrup, egg and vanilla; beat well. Stir together flour, baking soda and salt; gradually add to butter mixture, beating until well blended. Stir in any flavor Bake Shoppe pieces. Drop by rounded teaspoons onto ungreased cookie sheet.

3. Bake 8 to 10 minutes or until lightly browned and almost set. Cool slightly; remove from cookie sheet to wire rack. Cool completely. Cookies will be softer the second day. *About 3½ dozen cookies*

CHOCOLATE CHOCOLATE COOKIES: Decrease flour to 2¼ cups and add ¼ cup HERSHEY'S Cocoa or HERSHEY'S European Style Cocoa.

Hershey's Soft & Chewy Cookies

COCOA-CHIP COOKIES

⅔ cup shortening
1½ cups sugar
2 eggs
⅔ cup dairy sour cream
1 teaspoon vanilla extract
2 cups all-purpose flour
½ cup HERSHEY'S Cocoa or
    HERSHEY'S European
    Style Cocoa

½ teaspoon baking soda
½ teaspoon salt
2 cups (12-ounce package)
    HERSHEY'S MINICHIPS
    Semi-Sweet Chocolate

1. Heat oven to 375°F. Lightly grease cookie sheet.

2. In large bowl, beat shortening and sugar until blended. Add eggs, sour cream and vanilla; beat well. Stir together flour, cocoa, baking soda and salt; gradually add to shortening mixture, beating until well blended. Stir in small chocolate chips. Drop by teaspoons onto prepared cookie sheet.

3. Bake 8 to 10 minutes or until puffed and slightly cracked. Remove from cookie sheet to wire rack. Cool completely.   *About 5½ dozen cookies*

REESE'S CHEWY CHOCOLATE COOKIES

2 cups all-purpose flour
¾ cup HERSHEY'S Cocoa
1 teaspoon baking soda
½ teaspoon salt
1¼ cups (2½ sticks) butter
    or margarine, softened

2 cups sugar
2 eggs
2 teaspoons vanilla extract
1⅔ cups (10-ounce
    package) REESE'S
    Peanut Butter Chips

1. Heat oven to 350°F.

2. Stir together flour, cocoa, baking soda and salt. In large bowl, beat butter and sugar with electric mixer until light and fluffy. Add eggs and vanilla; beat well. Gradually add flour mixture, beating until well blended. Stir in peanut butter chips. Drop by rounded teaspoons onto ungreased cookie sheet.

3. Bake 8 to 9 minutes. (Do not overbake; cookies will be soft. They will puff while baking and flatten while cooling.) Cool slightly; remove from cookie sheet to wire rack. Cool completely.   *About 4¹/₂ dozen cookies*

PAN RECIPE: Spread batter into greased 15½ × 10½ × 1-inch jelly-roll pan. Bake at 350°F 20 minutes or until set. Cool completely in pan on wire rack; cut into bars.   *About 48 bars*

HIGH ALTITUDE DIRECTIONS: Increase flour to 2 cups plus 2 tablespoons. Decrease baking soda to ¾ teaspoon. Decrease sugar to 1⅔ cups. Add 2 teaspoons water with flour mixture. Bake at 350°F 7 to 8 minutes. Yield increases to about 6 dozen.

HERSHEY'S CHOCOLATE MINT BROWNIES

¾ **cup HERSHEY'S Cocoa**
½ **teaspoon baking soda**
⅔ **cup butter or margarine,**
     melted and divided
½ **cup boiling water**
2 **cups sugar**
2 **eggs**
1⅓ **cups all-purpose flour**

1 **teaspoon vanilla extract**
¼ **teaspoon salt**
1⅔ **cups (10-ounce**
     package) HERSHEY'S
     Mint Chocolate Chips
     Glaze (recipe follows),
     optional

1. Heat oven to 350°F. Grease 13 × 9 × 2-inch baking pan.

2. In large bowl, stir together cocoa and baking soda; stir in ⅓ cup butter. Add water; stir until mixture thickens. Stir in sugar, eggs and remaining ⅓ cup butter; stir until smooth. Add flour, vanilla and salt; stir until well blended. Stir in mint chocolate chips. Spread batter into prepared pan.

3. Bake 35 to 40 minutes or until brownies begin to pull away from sides of pan. Cool completely in pan on wire rack. Drizzle with Glaze, if desired. Cut into bars.   *About 36 brownies*

GLAZE: In small bowl, combine ⅔ cup powdered sugar and 2 to 3 teaspoons milk; stir in few drops green food color, if desired.

CHIPPY CHEWY BARS

½ cup (1 stick) butter or margarine

1½ cups graham cracker crumbs

1⅔ cups (10-ounce package) REESE'S Peanut Butter Chips, divided

1½ cups MOUNDS Sweetened Coconut Flakes

1 can (14 ounces) sweetened condensed milk (not evaporated milk)

1 cup HERSHEY'S Semi-Sweet Chocolate Chips or HERSHEY'S MINICHIPS Semi-Sweet Chocolate

1½ teaspoons shortening (do not use butter, margarine or oil)

1. Heat oven to 350°F.

2. Place butter in 13×9×2-inch baking pan. Heat in oven until melted. Remove pan from oven. Sprinkle graham cracker crumbs evenly over butter; press down with fork. Layer 1 cup peanut butter chips over crumbs; sprinkle coconut over peanut butter chips. Layer remaining ⅔ cup peanut butter chips over coconut; drizzle sweetened condensed milk evenly over top.

3. Bake 20 minutes or until lightly browned.

4. In small microwave-safe bowl, place chocolate chips and shortening. Microwave at HIGH (100%) 1 minute; stir. If necessary, microwave at HIGH an additional 15 seconds at a time, stirring after each heating, just until chips are melted when stirred. Drizzle evenly over top of baked mixture. Cool completely in pan on wire rack. Cut into bars. *About 48 bars*

NOTE: For lighter drizzle, use ½ cup chocolate chips and ¾ teaspoon shortening. Microwave at HIGH 30 seconds to 1 minute; stir. If necessary, microwave at HIGH an additional 15 seconds at a time, stirring after each heating, just until chips are melted when stirred.

Chippy Chewy Bars

OATMEAL BUTTERSCOTCH COOKIES

¾ cup (1½ sticks) butter
   or margarine, softened
¾ cup granulated sugar
¾ cup packed light brown
   sugar
2 eggs
1 teaspoon vanilla extract
1¼ cups all-purpose flour
1 teaspoon baking soda

½ teaspoon ground
   cinnamon
½ teaspoon salt
3 cups quick-cooking or
   regular rolled oats
1⅔ cups (10-ounce
   package) HERSHEY'S
   Butterscotch Chips

1. Heat oven to 375°F.

2. In large bowl, beat butter, granulated sugar and brown sugar until well blended. Add eggs and vanilla; blend thoroughly. Stir together flour, baking soda, cinnamon and salt; gradually add to butter mixture, beating until well blended. Stir in oats and butterscotch chips; mix well. Drop by teaspoons onto ungreased cookie sheet.

3. Bake 8 to 10 minutes or until golden brown. Cool slightly; remove from cookie sheet to wire rack. Cool completely.   *About 4 dozen cookies*

 TIP

To get the number of cookies listed in a drop cookie recipe, drop cookie dough with a tableware spoon, not a measuring spoon.

Oatmeal Butterscotch Cookies

HERSHEY'S CLASSIC MILK CHOCOLATE CHIP COOKIES

1 cup (2 sticks) butter, softened
¾ cup granulated sugar
¾ cup packed light brown sugar
1 teaspoon vanilla extract
2 eggs
2¼ cups all-purpose flour

1 teaspoon baking soda
½ teaspoon salt
2 cups (11.5-ounce package) HERSHEY'S Milk Chocolate Chips
1 cup chopped nuts (optional)

1. Heat oven to 375°F.

2. In large bowl, beat butter, granulated sugar, brown sugar and vanilla. Add eggs; beat well. Stir together flour, baking soda and salt; gradually add to butter mixture, beating until well blended. Stir in chocolate chips and nuts, if desired. Drop by teaspoons onto ungreased cookie sheet.

3. Bake 8 to 10 minutes or until lightly browned. Cool slightly; remove from cookie sheet to wire rack. Cool completely.   *About 5 dozen cookies*

PAN RECIPE: Spread batter into greased 15½ × 10½ × 1-inch jelly-roll pan. Bake at 375°F 20 minutes or until lightly browned. Cool completely. Cut into bars.   *About 48 bars*

FIVE LAYER BARS

¾ cup (1½ sticks) butter or margarine
1¾ cups graham cracker crumbs
¼ cup HERSHEY'S Cocoa
2 tablespoons sugar
1 can (14 ounces) sweetened condensed milk (not evaporated milk)

1 cup HERSHEY'S Semi-Sweet Chocolate Chips
1 cup raisins, chopped dried apricots or miniature marshmallows
1 cup chopped nuts

1. Heat oven to 350°F. Place butter in 13 × 9 × 2-inch baking pan. Heat in oven until melted. Remove pan from oven.

2. Stir together graham cracker crumbs, cocoa and sugar; sprinkle evenly over butter. Pour sweetened condensed milk evenly over crumb mixture. Sprinkle with chocolate chips and raisins. Sprinkle nuts on top; press down firmly.

3. Bake 25 to 30 minutes or until lightly browned. Cool completely in pan on wire rack. Cover with foil; let stand at room temperature 6 to 8 hours. Cut into bars. *About 36 bars*

VARIATION: Substitute 1 cup REESE'S Peanut Butter Chips for chocolate chips. Sprinkle 1 cup golden raisins or chopped dried apricots over chips. Proceed as above.

PEANUT BUTTER CHIP OATMEAL COOKIES

1 cup (2 sticks) butter or margarine, softened
¼ cup shortening
2 cups packed light brown sugar
1 tablespoon milk
2 teaspoons vanilla extract
1 egg
2 cups all-purpose flour

1⅔ cups (10-ounce package) REESE'S Peanut Butter Chips
1½ cups quick-cooking or regular rolled oats
½ cup chopped walnuts
½ teaspoon baking soda
½ teaspoon salt

1. Heat oven to 375°F.

2. In large bowl, beat butter, shortening, brown sugar, milk, vanilla and egg until well blended. Mix in remaining ingredients. Drop dough by rounded teaspoons about 2 inches apart onto ungreased cookie sheet.

3. Bake 10 to 12 minutes for soft cookies, 12 to 14 minutes for crisp cookies or until lightly browned. Remove from cookie sheet to wire rack. Cool completely. Store tightly covered. *About 6 dozen cookies*

CHOCOLATE CHIP 'N OATMEAL COOKIES

1 package (about 18 ounces) yellow cake mix
1 cup quick-cooking rolled oats
¾ cup (1½ sticks) butter or margarine, softened
2 eggs
1 cup HERSHEY'S Semi-Sweet Chocolate Chips

1. Heat oven to 350°F.

2. In large bowl, stir together cake mix, oats, butter and eggs; beat until well blended. Stir in chocolate chips. Drop by rounded teaspoons onto ungreased cookie sheet.

3. Bake 10 to 12 minutes or until very lightly browned. Cool slightly; remove from cookie sheet to wire rack. Cool completely.   *About 4 dozen cookies*

MOLASSES SNAPS

2¼ cups all-purpose flour
2 teaspoons baking soda
1 cup packed light brown sugar
¾ cup (1½ sticks) butter or margarine, softened
1 egg
¼ cup light molasses
1⅔ cups (10-ounce package) REESE'S Peanut Butter Chips
Granulated sugar

1. Stir together flour and baking soda. In large bowl, beat brown sugar and butter; add egg and molasses, beating until smooth. Stir in flour mixture and peanut butter chips until well blended. Cover; refrigerate 1 hour.

2. Heat oven to 350°F. Grease and flour cookie sheet.

3. Shape dough into 1-inch balls; roll in granulated sugar. Place on prepared cookie sheet.

4. Bake 8 to 10 minutes or until tops begin cracking; immediately remove from cookie sheet to wire rack. Cool completely.   *About 5 dozen cookies*

Chocolate Chip 'n Oatmeal Cookies

PEANUT BUTTER CUT-OUT COOKIES

½ cup (1 stick) butter or margarine
1 cup REESE'S Peanut Butter Chips
⅔ cup packed light brown sugar
1 egg
¾ teaspoon vanilla extract

1⅓ cups all-purpose flour
¾ teaspoon baking soda
½ cup finely chopped pecans
CHOCOLATE CHIP GLAZE or PEANUT BUTTER CHIP GLAZE (recipes follow)

1. In medium saucepan, combine butter and peanut butter chips; cook over low heat, stirring constantly, until melted. Pour into large bowl; add brown sugar, egg and vanilla, beating until well blended. Stir in flour, baking soda and pecans; blend well. Refrigerate 15 to 20 minutes or until firm enough to roll.

2. Heat oven to 350°F.

3. Roll out dough, a small portion at a time, on lightly floured surface or between 2 pieces of wax paper, to ¼-inch thickness. (Keep remaining dough in refrigerator.) With cookie cutters, cut into desired shapes; place on ungreased cookie sheet.

4. Bake 7 to 8 minutes or until almost set (do not overbake). Cool 1 minute; remove from cookie sheet to wire rack. Cool completely. Drizzle CHOCOLATE CHIP GLAZE or PEANUT BUTTER CHIP GLAZE onto each cookie.

About 3 dozen cookies

CHOCOLATE CHIP GLAZE: In small microwave-safe bowl, place 1 cup HERSHEY'S Semi-Sweet Chocolate Chips and 1 tablespoon shortening (do not use butter, margarine or oil). Microwave at HIGH (100%) 1 minute; stir. If necessary, microwave at HIGH an additional 15 seconds at a time, stirring after each heating, just until chips are melted when stirred.

About ⅔ cup glaze

continued on page 28

Peanut Butter Cut-Out Cookies

Peanut Butter Cut-Out Cookies, continued

PEANUT BUTTER CHIP GLAZE: In small microwave-safe bowl, place ⅔ cup REESE'S Peanut Butter Chips and 1 tablespoon shortening (do not use butter, margarine or oil). Microwave at HIGH (100%) 30 seconds; stir. Microwave at HIGH an additional 15 seconds at a time, stirring after each heating, just until chips are melted when stirred.   *About ⅓ cup glaze*

VARIATION: Prepare dough as directed above. Refrigerate 15 to 20 minutes or until firm enough to handle. Shape dough into two 6-inch rolls. Wrap rolls in wax paper or plastic wrap; freeze 1 to 2 hours or until firm enough to cut. Cut dough into ¼-inch thick slices. Proceed as directed for baking and cooling.

DOUBLE CHOCOLATE BROWNIE BARS

½ cup (1 stick) butter or margarine
2 cups (12-ounce package) HERSHEY'S Semi-Sweet Chocolate Chips, divided
1½ cups sugar
1¼ cups all-purpose flour
1 teaspoon vanilla extract
½ teaspoon baking powder
½ teaspoon salt
3 eggs
1 cup coarsely chopped walnuts

1. Heat oven to 350°F. Grease 13 × 9 × 2-inch baking pan.

2. In large microwave-safe bowl, place butter and 1 cup chocolate chips. Microwave at HIGH (100%) 1 to 1½ minutes or until chips are melted when stirred. Add sugar, flour, vanilla, baking powder, salt and eggs; stir with spoon until smooth. Stir in remaining 1 cup chips. Spread batter into prepared pan; sprinkle walnuts over top.

3. Bake 30 minutes or until center is set. Cool completely in pan on wire rack. Cut into bars. Store tightly covered.   *About 36 brownies*

VARIATION: Cut brownies into 3 × 3¼-inch squares. Serve topped with scoop of ice cream, fruit and chocolate syrup.

About 12 dessert squares

HERSHEY'S CLASSIC CHOCOLATE CHIP COOKIES

2¼ cups all-purpose flour
1 teaspoon baking soda
½ teaspoon salt
1 cup (2 sticks) butter, softened
¾ cup granulated sugar
¾ cup packed light brown sugar

1 teaspoon vanilla extract
2 eggs
2 cups (12-ounce package) HERSHEY'S Semi-Sweet Chocolate Chips
1 cup chopped nuts (optional)

1. Heat oven to 375°F.

2. Stir together flour, baking soda and salt. In large bowl, beat butter, granulated sugar, brown sugar and vanilla with electric mixer until creamy. Add eggs; beat well. Gradually add flour mixture, beating well. Stir in chocolate chips and nuts, if desired. Drop by rounded teaspoons onto ungreased cookie sheet.

3. Bake 8 to 10 minutes or until lightly browned. Cool slightly; remove from cookie sheet to wire rack. Cool completely.   *About 5 dozen cookies*

"PERFECTLY CHOCOLATE" CHOCOLATE CHIP COOKIES: Add ⅓ cup HERSHEY'S Cocoa to flour mixture.

PAN RECIPE: Spread batter into greased 15½ × 10½ × 1-inch jelly-roll pan. Bake at 375°F 20 minutes or until lightly browned. Cool completely. Cut into bars.   *About 48 bars*

ICE CREAM SANDWICH: Press one small scoop of vanilla ice cream between two cookies.

HIGH ALTITUDE DIRECTIONS: Increase flour to 2⅔ cups. Decrease baking soda to ¾ teaspoon. Decrease granulated sugar to ⅔ cup. Decrease packed light brown sugar to ⅔ cup. Add ½ teaspoon water with flour. Bake at 375°F 5 to 7 minutes or until top is light golden with golden brown edges.

KIDS' KITCHEN

PEANUT BUTTER CHIPS AND JELLY BARS

1½ cups all-purpose flour
½ cup sugar
¾ teaspoon baking powder
½ cup (1 stick) cold butter
  or margarine
1 egg, beaten

¾ cup grape jelly
1⅔ cups (10-ounce
  package) REESE'S
  Peanut Butter Chips,
  divided

1. Heat oven to 375°F. Grease 9-inch square baking pan.

2. Stir together flour, sugar and baking powder. Cut in butter with pastry blender until mixture resembles coarse crumbs. Add egg; blend well. Reserve one-half of mixture; press remaining mixture onto bottom of prepared pan. Spread jelly evenly over crust. Sprinkle 1 cup peanut butter chips over jelly. Stir together remaining crumb mixture with remaining ⅔ cup chips; sprinkle over top.

3. Bake 25 to 30 minutes or until lightly browned. Cool completely in pan on wire rack. Cut into bars.   *About 16 bars*

HIGH ALTITUDE DIRECTIONS: Increase flour to 1½ cups plus 1 tablespoon. Add 1 tablespoon water with egg. Do not change baking time or temperature.

Peanut Butter Chips and Jelly Bars

REESE'S BITS BLONDIES

⅔ cup butter or margarine,
   softened
1 cup packed light brown
   sugar
½ cup granulated sugar
¾ cup REESE'S Creamy or
   REESE'S Crunchy
   Peanut Butter
2 eggs
1 teaspoon vanilla extract

⅓ cup milk
1¾ cups all-purpose flour
1 teaspoon baking powder
1⅓ cups (10-ounce
   package) REESE'S Bits
   for Baking, divided
   CHOCOLATE BROWNIE
   FROSTING (recipe
   follows)

1. Heat oven to 325°F. Grease 13 × 9 × 2-inch baking pan.

2. In large bowl, beat butter, brown sugar, granulated sugar and peanut butter until creamy. Add eggs and vanilla; beat well. Gradually beat in milk. Gradually beat in flour and baking powder, beating thoroughly. Stir in 1 cup baking bits. Spread batter into prepared pan.

3. Bake 40 to 45 minutes or until wooden pick inserted in center comes out clean. Cool completely in pan on wire rack. Meanwhile, prepare CHOCOLATE BROWNIE FROSTING; spread over top of blondies. Sprinkle remaining ⅓ cup bits on top. Cut into bars.   *About 36 bars*

CHOCOLATE BROWNIE FROSTING

¼ cup (½ stick) butter or
   margarine, softened
¼ cup HERSHEY'S Cocoa
1 tablespoon light corn
   syrup

2 tablespoons milk
1 teaspoon vanilla extract
1½ cups powdered sugar

1. In medium bowl, beat butter, cocoa, corn syrup, milk and vanilla until smooth. Gradually add powdered sugar, beating until spreading consistency.
                                   About 1¼ cups frosting

Reese's Bits Blondies

SUGAR DOODLES

1 package (22.3 ounces) golden sugar cookie mix
2 eggs
⅓ cup oil
1 teaspoon water
½ cup (of each) HERSHEY'S Butterscotch Chips,
HERSHEY'S Semi-Sweet Chocolate Chips and REESE'S Peanut Butter Chips
5 tablespoons colored sugar
1 tablespoon granulated sugar

1. Heat oven to 375°F.

2. Empty cookie mix into large bowl. Break up any lumps. Add eggs, oil and water to mix; stir with spoon or fork until well blended. Stir in butterscotch chips, chocolate chips and peanut butter chips. Cover; refrigerate dough about 1 hour.

3. Shape dough into 1½-inch balls. Place colored sugar and granulated sugar in large reclosable plastic bag; shake well to blend. Place 2 balls into bag; reclose bag and shake well. Place balls 2 inches apart on ungreased cookie sheet. Repeat until all balls are coated with sugar mixture.

4. Bake 8 to 10 minutes or until set. Cool slightly; remove from cookie sheet to wire rack. Cool completely. *About 2½ dozen cookies*

COCOA SUGAR DOODLES: Substitute 5 tablespoons granulated sugar and ¾ teaspoon HERSHEY'S Cocoa or HERSHEY'S European Style Cocoa for amounts of colored and granulated sugars above.

RAINBOW SUGAR DOODLES: Substitute about 1¾ teaspoons each of blue, pink and yellow colored sugar for the 5 tablespoons colored sugar called for above.

THREE-IN-ONE CHOCOLATE CHIP COOKIES

6 tablespoons butter or margarine, softened
½ cup packed light brown sugar
¼ cup granulated sugar
1 egg
1 teaspoon vanilla extract

1½ cups all-purpose flour
½ teaspoon baking soda
¼ teaspoon salt
2 cups (12-ounce package) HERSHEY'S Semi-Sweet Chocolate Chips

1. In large bowl, beat butter, brown sugar and granulated sugar until light and fluffy. Add egg and vanilla; beat well. Stir together flour, baking soda and salt; gradually blend into butter mixture. Stir in chocolate chips. Shape and bake cookies into one of the three versions below:

GIANT COOKIES: Prepare dough. Heat oven to 350°F. Line 12 × ⅝-inch round pizza pan with foil. Pat dough evenly into prepared pan to within ¾-inch of edge. Bake 15 to 18 minutes or until lightly browned. Cool completely; cut into wedges. Decorate or garnish as desired.

About 8 servings (one 12-inch cookie)

MEDIUM-SIZE REFRIGERATOR COOKIES: Prepare dough. On wax paper, shape into 2 rolls, 1½ inches in diameter. Wrap in wax paper; cover with plastic wrap. Refrigerate several hours, or until firm enough to slice. Heat oven to 350°F. Remove rolls from refrigerator; remove wrapping. With sharp knife, cut into ¼-inch wide slices. Place on ungreased cookie sheet, about 3 inches apart. Bake 8 to 10 minutes or until lightly browned. Cool slightly; remove from cookie sheet to wire rack. Cool completely. *About 2½ dozen (2½-inch cookies)*

MINIATURE COOKIES: Prepare dough. Heat oven to 350°F. Drop dough by ¼ teaspoons onto ungreased cookie sheet, about 1½ inches apart. (OR spoon dough into disposable plastic frosting bag; cut about ¼-inch off tip. Squeeze batter by ¼ teaspoons onto ungreased cookie sheet.) Bake 5 to 7 minutes or just until set. Cool slightly; remove from cookie sheet to wire rack. Cool completely.

About 18½ dozen (¾-inch) cookies

P.B. CHIPS BROWNIE CUPS

1 cup (2 sticks) butter or
   margarine
2 cups sugar
2 teaspoons vanilla extract
4 eggs
¾ cup HERSHEY'S Cocoa or
   HERSHEY'S European
   Style Cocoa

1¾ cups all-purpose flour
½ teaspoon baking powder
½ teaspoon salt
1⅔ cups (10-ounce
   package) REESE'S
   Peanut Butter Chips,
   divided

1. Heat oven to 350°F. Line 18 muffin cups (2½ inches in diameter) with paper or foil bake cups.

2. In large microwave-safe bowl, place butter. Microwave at HIGH (100%) 1 to 1½ minutes or until melted. Stir in sugar and vanilla. Add eggs; beat well. Add cocoa; beat until well blended. Add flour, baking powder and salt; beat well. Stir in 1⅓ cups peanut butter chips. Divide batter evenly into muffin cups; sprinkle with remaining ⅓ cup peanut butter chips.

3. Bake 25 to 30 minutes or until surface is firm; cool completely in pan on wire rack.
About 1½ dozen brownie cups

 TIP

Butter and margarine are interchangeable if both are listed in the ingredient list. Do not use low-fat spreads, soft or tub margarine unless the recipe specifically calls for these ingredients. They act differently and may cause unsatisfactory results.

P.B. Chips Brownie Cups

HALLOWEEN COOKIE PIZZA

¾ cup packed light brown
   sugar
½ cup butter flavor
   shortening
1 egg
1 tablespoon water
1 teaspoon vanilla extract
1¼ cups all-purpose flour
½ teaspoon baking soda
¼ teaspoon salt
1 cup REESE'S Peanut
   Butter Chips

1 cup miniature
   marshmallows
½ cup HERSHEY'S Semi-
   Sweet Chocolate Chips
½ cup chopped pecans
CHOCOLATE DRIZZLE
   (recipe follows)
ORANGE DRIZZLE
   (recipe follows)

1. Heat oven to 350°F. Lightly grease 12-inch round pizza pan.

2. In large bowl, beat brown sugar and shortening until creamy. Add egg, water and vanilla; beat well. Stir together flour, baking soda and salt; add to sugar mixture, beating on low speed of electric mixer until well blended. Stir in peanut butter chips. Spread batter into prepared pan to within ½ inch of edge.

3. Bake 11 to 13 minutes or until set. Remove from oven. Sprinkle marshmallows, chocolate chips and pecans over top. Return to oven. Bake 5 to 7 minutes or until marshmallows are lightly browned. Cool completely.

4. Prepare CHOCOLATE DRIZZLE and ORANGE DRIZZLE. Drizzle CHOCOLATE DRIZZLE over top. Drizzle ORANGE DRIZZLE over chocolate. Let stand about 1 hour until drizzles set. Cut into wedges. *About 16 to 20 servings*

CHOCOLATE DRIZZLE: In small microwave-safe bowl, place ¼ cup HERSHEY'S Semi-Sweet Chocolate Chips and 1½ teaspoons butter flavor shortening. Microwave at MEDIUM (50%) 1 minute; stir. If necessary, microwave at MEDIUM an additional 15 seconds at a time, stirring after each heating, just until chips are melted when stirred.

ORANGE DRIZZLE: In small bowl, stir together ½ cup powdered sugar, 1 tablespoon water, 3 drops yellow food color and 2 drops red food color; stir until well blended.

Halloween Cookie Pizza

CHOCOLATE PEANUT BUTTER THUMBPRINTS

1⅔ cups (10-ounce package) REESE'S Peanut Butter Chips, divided
½ cup (1 stick) butter or margarine, softened
½ cup granulated sugar
½ cup packed light brown sugar

1 egg
1 teaspoon vanilla extract
1½ cups all-purpose flour
½ cup HERSHEY'S Cocoa or HERSHEY'S European Style Cocoa
½ teaspoon baking soda
Additional granulated sugar

1. Heat oven to 375°F.

2. In small microwave-safe bowl, place ½ cup peanut butter chips. Microwave at HIGH (100%) 30 to 40 seconds or just until chips are melted and smooth when stirred; set aside.

3. In large bowl, beat butter, ½ cup granulated sugar, brown sugar, egg and vanilla until light and fluffy. Add melted peanut butter chips; beat well. Stir together flour, cocoa and baking soda; stir into peanut butter mixture until well blended.

4. For each cookie, shape 1 tablespoon dough into ball; roll in additional granulated sugar. Place balls on ungreased cookie sheet. With bottom of glass, flatten cookies to ¼-inch thickness. Using thumb, make indentation in center of each cookie.

5. Bake 6 to 8 minutes or just until set. Remove from oven. If necessary, using tip of spoon, press indentation in center of each cookie; immediately place 1 teaspoonful peanut butter chips in each indentation. After several minutes, swirl melted peanut butter chips in each thumbprint. Remove from cookie sheet to wire rack. Cool completely. *About 2½ dozen cookies*

CHEWY ROCKY ROAD BARS

1½ cups finely crushed
    unsalted pretzels
¾ cup (1½ sticks) butter
    or margarine, melted
1 can (14 ounces)
    sweetened condensed
    milk (not evaporated
    milk)
2 cups miniature
    marshmallows

1 cup HERSHEY'S
    Butterscotch Chips
1 cup HERSHEY'S Semi-
    Sweet Chocolate Chips
1 cup MOUNDS Sweetened
    Coconut Flakes
¾ cup chopped nuts

1. Heat oven to 350°F.

2. In small bowl, combine crushed pretzels and butter; lightly press mixture into bottom of 13 × 9 × 2-inch baking pan. Pour sweetened condensed milk evenly over crumb mixture. Top with marshmallows, butterscotch chips, chocolate chips, coconut and nuts. Press toppings firmly into sweetened condensed milk.

3. Bake 25 to 30 minutes or until lightly browned. Cool completely in pan on wire rack. Cut into bars. *About 36 bars*

VARIATIONS: 2 cups (12-ounce package) HERSHEY'S Semi-Sweet Chocolate Chips OR 1⅔ cups (10-ounce package) HERSHEY'S Butterscotch Chips may be used instead of 1 cup of each flavor.

BROWNIES WITH PEANUT BUTTER CHIPS

1¼ cups (2½ sticks) butter
   or margarine, melted
1¾ cups sugar
 4 eggs
 2 teaspoons vanilla extract
1⅔ cups all-purpose flour
 ⅔ cup HERSHEY'S Cocoa
 ½ teaspoon baking powder

½ teaspoon salt
1⅔ cups (10-ounce
   package) REESE'S
   Peanut Butter Chips,
   divided
PEANUT BUTTER CHIP
   GLAZE (recipe follows)

1. Heat oven to 350°F. Grease 13×9×2-inch baking pan.

2. In large bowl, stir together butter and sugar. Add eggs and vanilla; beat with spoon or whisk until well blended. Stir together flour, cocoa, baking powder and salt; add to butter mixture, stirring until well blended. Reserve ½ cup peanut butter chips for glaze. Stir remaining chips into batter. Spread batter into prepared pan.

3. Bake 30 to 35 minutes or until wooden pick inserted in center comes out clean. Cool completely in pan on wire rack. Meanwhile, prepare PEANUT BUTTER CHIP GLAZE; drizzle over brownies. Let stand until glaze is set. Cut into squares.   *About 32 brownies*

PEANUT BUTTER CHIP GLAZE: In small microwave-safe bowl, place ½ cup REESE'S Peanut Butter Chips (reserved from brownies), 2 tablespoons butter or margarine and 2 tablespoons milk. Microwave at HIGH (100%) 45 seconds; stir. If necessary, microwave at HIGH an additional 15 seconds at a time, stirring after each heating, just until chips are melted when stirred. Gradually add ¼ cup powdered sugar, beating with whisk until smooth.

Brownies with Peanut Butter Chips

BUTTERSCOTCH BLONDIES

¾ cup (1½ sticks) butter
   or margarine, softened
¾ cup packed light brown
   sugar
½ cup granulated sugar
2 eggs
2 cups all-purpose flour

1 teaspoon baking soda
½ teaspoon salt
1⅔ cups (10-ounce
   package) HERSHEY'S
   Butterscotch Chips
1 cup chopped nuts
   (optional)

1. Heat oven to 350°F. Grease 13×9×2-inch baking pan.

2. In large bowl, beat butter, brown sugar and granulated sugar until light and fluffy. Add eggs; beat until well blended. Stir together flour, baking soda and salt; gradually add to butter mixture, mixing well. Stir in butterscotch chips and nuts, if desired. Spread into prepared pan.

3. Bake 30 to 35 minutes or until golden brown and center is set. Cool completely in pan on wire rack. Cut into bars. *About 36 bars*

 TIP

Shiny pans and cookie sheets are preferred for baking cookies and bars since they reflect heat and will produce light, delicate crusts.

Butterscotch Blondies

EASY BAKE SHOPPE MARBLED BROWNIES

⅔ cup all-purpose flour
¼ teaspoon baking soda
¼ teaspoon salt
½ cup sugar
   2 tablespoons butter or margarine
   2 tablespoons water

1⅔ cups HERSHEY'S Semi-Sweet Chocolate Chips, divided
   2 eggs, slightly beaten
   1 teaspoon vanilla extract
CREAM CHEESE MARBLE (recipe follows)

1. Heat oven to 350°F. Line 8-inch-square baking pan with foil; grease foil.

2. Stir together flour, baking soda and salt. In medium saucepan, place sugar, butter and water. Cook over low heat, stirring constantly, until mixture comes to boil. Remove from heat. Immediately add 1 cup chocolate chips, stirring until melted. Stir in eggs and vanilla until blended; gradually add flour mixture, blending well. Spread ⅔ of chocolate batter into prepared pan.

3. Prepare CREAM CHEESE MARBLE. Spoon over chocolate; drop spoonfuls of remaining chocolate batter onto cream cheese mixture. Gently swirl chocolate batter into cream cheese with spatula.

4. Bake 35 to 40 minutes or until brownies begin to pull away from sides of pan. Cool completely in pan on wire rack. Remove from pan; peel off foil. Cut into squares.   *About 18 brownies*

CREAM CHEESE MARBLE: In small bowl, beat 1 package (3 ounces) softened cream cheese and ¼ cup sugar until smooth. Add 1 egg and ½ teaspoon vanilla extract; beat well. Stir in remaining ⅔ cup chocolate chips.

RASPBERRY VARIATION: Substitute 1⅔ cups (10-ounce package) HERSHEY'S Raspberry Chips for semi-sweet chips. Add 2 drops red food color to CREAM CHEESE MARBLE, if desired.

MINT VARIATION: Substitute 1⅔ cups (10-ounce package) HERSHEY'S Mint Chocolate Chips. Add 2 drops green food color to CREAM CHEESE MARBLE, if desired.

SOFT BANANA CHIP COOKIES

1 cup shortening
1½ cups sugar
2 eggs
1 teaspoon vanilla extract
2¾ cups all-purpose flour
1½ teaspoons baking soda
½ teaspoon salt
½ cup buttermilk or sour milk*
1 cup mashed ripe banana (3 medium)

1 cup chopped nuts
2 cups (12-ounce package) HERSHEY'S Semi-Sweet Chocolate Chips OR 2 cups (11.5-ounce package) HERSHEY'S Milk Chocolate Chips

1. Heat oven to 375°F. Lightly grease cookie sheet.

2. In large bowl, beat shortening and sugar until well blended. Add eggs and vanilla; beat well. Stir together flour, baking soda and salt; add alternately with buttermilk and banana to shortening mixture, beating until well blended. Stir in nuts and chocolate chips. (Dough will be soft.) Drop by teaspoons onto prepared cookie sheet.

3. Bake 8 to 10 minutes or until lightly browned. Cool slightly; remove from cookie sheet to wire rack. Cool completely. *About 7 dozen cookies*

To sour milk: Use 1½ teaspoons white vinegar plus enough milk to equal ½ cup.

 TIP

Crisp and soft cookies should be stored separately. Store soft cookies in containers with tight fitting lids. Store crisp cookies in containers with loose fitting lids. Store bar cookies in the pan in which they were baked and cover the pan with foil.

JOLLY PEANUT BUTTER GINGERBREAD COOKIES

1⅔ cups (10-ounce package) REESE'S Peanut Butter Chips
¾ cup (1½ sticks) butter or margarine, softened
1 cup packed light brown sugar
1 cup dark corn syrup

2 eggs
5 cups all-purpose flour
1 teaspoon baking soda
½ teaspoon ground cinnamon
¼ teaspoon ground ginger
¼ teaspoon salt

1. In small microwave-safe bowl, place peanut butter chips. Microwave at HIGH (100%) 1 to 2 minutes or until chips are melted when stirred. In large bowl, beat melted peanut butter chips and butter until well blended. Add brown sugar, corn syrup and eggs; beat until light and fluffy. Stir together flour, baking soda, cinnamon, ginger and salt. Add half of flour mixture to butter mixture; beat on low speed of electric mixer until smooth. With wooden spoon, stir in remaining flour mixture until well blended. Divide into thirds; wrap each in plastic wrap. Refrigerate at least 1 hour or until dough is firm enough to roll.

2. Heat oven to 325°F.

3. On lightly floured surface, roll 1 dough portion at a time to ⅛-inch thickness; with floured cookie cutters, cut into holiday shapes. Place on ungreased cookie sheet.

4. Bake 10 to 12 minutes or until set and lightly browned. Cool slightly; remove from cookie sheet to wire rack. Cool completely. Frost and decorate as desired.

About 6 dozen cookies

Jolly Peanut Butter Gingerbread Cookies

Treats with a Twist

PEANUT BUTTER CHIP PINEAPPLE DROPS

¼ cup (½ stick) butter or
    margarine, softened
¼ cup shortening
1 cup packed light brown
    sugar
1 egg
1 teaspoon vanilla extract
2 cups all-purpose flour
1 teaspoon baking powder
½ teaspoon baking soda

½ teaspoon salt
1 can (8 ounces) crushed
    pineapple, drained
1 cup REESE'S Peanut
    Butter Chips
½ cup chopped nuts
    (optional)
    Red candied cherries,
    halved

1. Heat oven to 375°F.

2. In large bowl, beat butter and shortening until blended. Add sugar, egg and vanilla; beat until fluffy. Stir together flour, baking powder, baking soda and salt; add to butter mixture, beating until well blended. Stir in pineapple, peanut butter chips and nuts, if desired. Drop by teaspoons onto ungreased cookie sheet. Lightly press cherry half in center of each cookie.

3. Bake 10 to 12 minutes or until lightly browned. Remove from cookie sheet to wire rack. Cool completely. *About 3½ dozen cookies*

Peanut Butter Chip Pineapple Drops

50

RICH CHOCOLATE CHIP TOFFEE BARS

2⅓ cups all-purpose flour
⅔ cup packed light brown
    sugar
¾ cup (1½ sticks) butter
    or margarine
1 egg, slightly beaten
2 cups (12-ounce
    package) HERSHEY'S
    Semi-Sweet Chocolate
    Chips, divided

1 cup coarsely chopped
    nuts
1 can (14 ounces)
    sweetened condensed
    milk (not evaporated
    milk)
1¾ cups (10-ounce
    package) SKOR
    English Toffee Bits,
    divided

1. Heat oven to 350°F. Grease 13 × 9 × 2-inch baking pan.

2. In large bowl, stir together flour and brown sugar. Cut in butter with pastry blender until mixture resembles coarse crumbs. Add egg; mix well. Stir in 1½ cups chocolate chips and nuts. Reserve 1½ cups mixture. Press remaining crumb mixture onto bottom of prepared pan.

3. Bake 10 minutes. Pour sweetened condensed milk evenly over hot crust. Top with 1½ cups toffee bits. Sprinkle reserved crumb mixture and remaining ½ cup chips over top.

4. Bake 25 to 30 minutes or until golden brown. Sprinkle with remaining ¼ cup toffee bits. Cool completely in pan on wire rack. Cut into bars.

About 36 bars

Rich Chocolate Chip Toffee Bars

PEANUT BUTTER CHEESECAKE BROWNIE BARS

PEANUT BUTTER CHEESECAKE FILLING (recipe follows)
1 cup HERSHEY'S Semi-Sweet Chocolate Chips, divided
½ cup (1 stick) butter or margarine, softened
1 cup sugar

1 egg
1 teaspoon vanilla extract
1¼ cups all-purpose flour
¼ cup HERSHEY'S Cocoa
½ teaspoon baking soda
¼ teaspoon salt
½ teaspoon shortening (do not use butter, margarine or oil)

1. Heat oven to 350°F.

2. Prepare PEANUT BUTTER CHEESECAKE FILLING.

3. Reserve 1 tablespoon chocolate chips for drizzle. In large bowl, beat butter, sugar, egg and vanilla until well blended. Stir together flour, cocoa, baking soda and salt; gradually add to butter mixture, beating until blended. Stir in remaining chips. Spread batter into 13 × 9 × 2-inch baking pan. Spread cheesecake filling over brownie batter.

4. Bake 25 to 30 minutes or until wooden pick inserted in center comes out clean. Cool completely in pan on wire rack.

5. Place reserved chips and shortening in small microwave-safe bowl. Microwave at HIGH (100%) 30 seconds or until chips are melted and smooth when stirred. Drizzle over surface. Cover; refrigerate until ready to serve. Cut into bars. Allow to soften slightly. Refrigerate leftover bars.   *About 36 bars*

PEANUT BUTTER CHEESECAKE FILLING

1 package (8 ounces) cream cheese, softened
½ cup REESE'S Creamy or REESE'S Crunchy Peanut Butter

½ cup sugar
1 tablespoon all-purpose flour
1 egg
1 teaspoon vanilla extract

1. In small bowl, beat cream cheese and peanut butter. Add sugar, flour, egg and vanilla; beat well.

TROPICAL GARDENS COOKIES

½ cup (1 stick) butter or
  margarine, softened
½ cup shortening
1 cup granulated sugar
¼ cup packed light brown
  sugar
1 teaspoon vanilla extract
1 egg
1 tablespoon freshly
  grated orange peel

2¾ cups all-purpose flour
1½ teaspoons baking soda
1 teaspoon salt
¼ cup orange juice
2 cups (12-ounce
  package) HERSHEY'S
  MINICHIPS Semi-Sweet
  Chocolate
Additional granulated
  sugar

1. In large bowl, beat butter, shortening, 1 cup granulated sugar, brown sugar and vanilla until light and fluffy. Add egg and orange peel; blend well. Stir together flour, baking soda and salt; add alternately with orange juice to butter mixture. Stir in small chocolate chips. Cover; refrigerate dough about 1 hour or until firm enough to handle.

2. Heat oven to 350°F.

3. Shape dough into 1-inch balls; roll in granulated sugar. Place on ungreased cookie sheet; flatten by crisscrossing with tines of fork.

4. Bake 8 to 10 minutes or until lightly browned. Cool slightly; remove from cookie sheet to wire rack. Cool completely.   *About 7 dozen cookies*

MINI KISSES PRALINE BARS

2 cups all-purpose flour
1⅓ cups packed light brown
**   sugar, divided**
½ cup (1 stick) plus ⅔ cup
**   butter, divided**

1 cup coarsely chopped
**   pecans**
1¾ cups (10-ounce
**   package) HERSHEY'S**
**   MINI KISSES Chocolate**

1. Heat oven to 350°F.

2. In large bowl, stir together flour and 1 cup brown sugar; cut in ½ cup butter with pastry blender until fine crumbs form. Press mixture into 13 × 9 × 2-inch baking pan; sprinkle with pecans.

3. In small saucepan, place remaining ⅔ cup butter and remaining ⅓ cup brown sugar; cook over medium heat, stirring constantly, until mixture boils. Continue boiling, stirring constantly, 30 seconds, until sugar dissolves; drizzle evenly over pecans and crust.

4. Bake 18 to 22 minutes until topping is bubbly and golden; remove from oven. Immediately sprinkle MINI KISSES Chocolate over top. Cool completely in pan on wire rack. Cut into bars. *About 36 bars*

 TIP

Bloom, the gray film that sometimes appears on chocolate and chocolate chips, occurs when chocolate is exposed to varying temperatures or has been stored in damp conditions. Bloom does not affect the taste or quality of the chocolate.

Mini Kisses Praline Bars

OATMEAL TOFFEE BARS

1 cup (2 sticks) butter or
   margarine, softened
½ cup packed light brown
   sugar
½ cup granulated sugar
2 eggs
1 teaspoon vanilla extract
1½ cups all-purpose flour
1 teaspoon baking soda

½ teaspoon ground
   cinnamon
½ teaspoon salt
3 cups quick-cooking or
   regular rolled oats
1¾ cups (10-ounce
   package) SKOR
   English Toffee bits,
   divided

1. Heat oven to 350°F. Grease 13 × 9 × 2-inch baking pan.

2. In large bowl, beat butter, brown sugar and granulated sugar until well blended. Add eggs and vanilla; beat well. Stir together flour, baking soda, cinnamon and salt; gradually add to butter mixture, beating until well blended. Stir in oats and 1⅓ cups toffee bits (mixture will be stiff). Spread mixture into prepared pan.

3. Bake 25 minutes or until wooden pick inserted in center comes out clean. Immediately sprinkle remaining toffee bits over surface. Cool completely in pan on wire rack. Cut into bars. *About 36 bars*

 TIP

Bar cookies can be cut into different shapes for variety. To cut into triangles, cut cookie bars into 2- to 3-inch squares, then diagonally cut each square in half. To make diamond shapes, cut parallel lines 2 inches apart across the length of the pan, then cut diagonal lines 2 inches apart.

Oatmeal Toffee Bars

ALMOND JOY BITS SUGAR COOKIES

½ cup shortening
¾ cup sugar
2 eggs
½ cup buttermilk or sour milk*
1 teaspoon vanilla extract
2 cups all-purpose flour
1 teaspoon baking powder

¾ teaspoon baking soda
1⅔ cups (10-ounce package) ALMOND JOY Coconut & Almond Bits
1 egg white, slightly beaten
Additional sugar

1. Heat oven to 375°F.

2. In large bowl, beat shortening and sugar until well blended. Add eggs, buttermilk and vanilla; beat well. Stir together flour, baking powder and baking soda; add to shortening mixture, beating until well blended. Stir in bits. Drop by tablespoons onto ungreased cookie sheet. Brush egg white over top; sprinkle lightly with sugar.

3. Bake 8 to 10 minutes or until lightly browned. Remove from cookie sheet to wire rack. Cool completely. *About 3 dozen cookies*

To sour milk: Use 1½ teaspoons white vinegar plus enough milk to equal ½ cup.

TOFFEE STUDDED SNICKERDOODLES

½ cup (1 stick) butter or margarine, softened
½ cup shortening
1 cup plus 3 tablespoons sugar, divided
2 eggs
2¾ cups all-purpose flour
2 teaspoons cream of tartar

1 teaspoon baking soda
¼ teaspoon salt
1¾ cups (10-ounce package) SKOR English Toffee Bits
1 teaspoon ground cinnamon

1. Heat oven to 400°F.

2. In large bowl, beat butter, shortening and 1 cup sugar until light and fluffy. Add eggs; beat thoroughly. Stir together flour, cream of tartar, baking soda and salt; gradually add to butter mixture, beating until well blended. Stir in toffee bits. Stir together remaining 3 tablespoons sugar and cinnamon. Shape dough into 1¼-inch balls; roll in sugar-cinnamon mixture. Place on ungreased cookie sheet.

3. Bake 9 to 11 minutes or until lightly browned around edges. Cool slightly; remove from cookie sheet to wire rack. Cool completely.

About 5 dozen cookies

FUDGEY RASPBERRY BROWNIES

1⅔ cups (10-ounce package) HERSHEY'S Raspberry Chips
½ cup (1 stick) butter or margarine
2 eggs
1 teaspoon vanilla extract
1 cup all-purpose flour
½ cup sugar
¼ teaspoon baking soda
½ cup coarsely chopped nuts (optional)

1. Heat oven to 350°F. Grease 8-inch square baking pan.

2. In medium saucepan, combine raspberry chips and butter. Cook over medium heat, stirring constantly, until melted. Remove from heat. Add eggs and vanilla; stir until well blended. Add flour, sugar and baking soda; stir until well blended. Stir in nuts, if desired. Spread batter into prepared pan.

3. Bake 25 to 30 minutes or until wooden pick inserted in center comes out almost clean. Cool completely in pan on wire rack. Cut into squares.

About 20 brownies

HERSHEY'S 50% REDUCED FAT OATMEAL CHIP COOKIES

¾ cup (1½ sticks) 56-60% vegetable oil spread, softened
¾ cup granulated sugar
¾ cup packed light brown sugar
2 eggs
1 teaspoon vanilla extract
1¼ cups all-purpose flour
1 teaspoon baking soda

½ to ¾ teaspoon ground cinnamon
½ teaspoon salt
2¾ cups quick-cooking rolled oats
2 cups (12-ounce package) HERSHEY'S Reduced Fat Semi-Sweet Baking Chips
1 cup raisins

1. Heat oven to 375°F.

2. In large bowl, beat vegetable oil spread, granulated sugar and brown sugar with electric mixer until well mixed. Add eggs and vanilla; beat until creamy. Stir together flour, baking soda, cinnamon and salt; gradually add to sugar mixture, mixing well. Stir in oats, chips and raisins. Drop by teaspoons onto ungreased cookie sheet.

3. Bake 8 to 10 minutes or until golden brown. Cool slightly; remove from cookie sheet to wire rack. Cool completely.
4 dozen cookies

NUTRITIONAL INFORMATION PER SERVING: 1 Cookie
110 Calories (25 Calories from Fat), 3.5 g Total Fat‡ (5% Daily Value), 1.5 g Saturated Fat (8% Daily Value), 10 mg Cholesterol (3% Daily Value), 70 mg Sodium (3% Daily Value), 19 g Total Carbohydrate (6% Daily Value), 1 g Dietary Fiber (4% Daily Value), 13 g Sugars, 2 g Protein, 2% Daily Value Vitamin A, 0% Daily Value Vitamin C, 0% Daily Value Calcium, 2% Daily Value Iron.

‡ Contains 1 g of Salatrim per serving, only 55% of which is used by the body. Therefore this recipe provides 3 g of available total fat per serving vs. 6 g in the OATMEAL BUTTERSCOTCH COOKIES recipe.

Hershey's 50% Reduced Fat Oatmeal Chip Cookies

HERSHEY'S 50% REDUCED FAT FORGOTTEN CHIPS COOKIES

2 egg whites
⅛ teaspoon cream of tartar
⅛ teaspoon salt
⅔ cup sugar

1 cup HERSHEY'S Reduced Fat Semi-Sweet Baking Chips
1 teaspoon vanilla extract

1. Heat oven to 375°F. Lightly spray cookie sheet with non-stick vegetable cooking spray.

2. In small bowl, beat egg whites with cream of tartar and salt until soft peaks form; gradually add sugar, beating until stiff peaks form. Carefully fold in chips and vanilla. Drop by teaspoons onto prepared cookie sheet.

3. Place cookie sheet in preheated oven; immediately turn off oven and allow cookies to remain 6 hours or overnight, without opening door. Remove cookies from cookie sheet. Store in airtight container in cool, dry place.

2½ dozen cookies

NUTRITIONAL INFORMATION PER SERVING: 2 Cookies

90 Calories (15 Calories from Fat), 2.5 g Total Fat‡ (4% Daily Value), 2.5 g Saturated Fat (13% Daily Value), 0 mg Cholesterol (0% Daily Value), 25 mg Sodium (1% Daily Value), 17 g Total Carbohydrate (6% Daily Value), <1 g Dietary Fiber (3% Daily Value), 15 g Sugars, 1 g Protein, 0% Daily Value Vitamin A, 0% Daily Value Vitamin C, 0% Daily Value Calcium, 0% Daily Value Iron.

‡ Contains 2.5 g of Salatrim per serving, only 55% of which is used by the body. Therefore this recipe provides 1.5 g of available total fat per serving vs. 3.5 g in the FORGOTTEN CHIPS COOKIES recipe.

Hershey's 50% Reduced Fat Forgotten Chips Cookies

LAYERED APRICOT SNACKING BARS

1⅔ cups (10-ounce package) HERSHEY'S Premier White Chips, divided
1 package (6 ounces) dried apricots, cut into ¼-inch pieces
1 cup boiling water
½ cup (1 stick) margarine, softened
⅓ cup granulated sugar
¼ cup packed light brown sugar
1 teaspoon vanilla extract
1 cup plus 2 tablespoons all-purpose flour, divided
¼ teaspoon baking soda
¼ teaspoon salt
½ cup wheat germ
2 tablespoons honey
1 egg white
½ teaspoon shortening

1. Heat oven to 350°F.

2. Measure ⅓ cup white chips for glaze; set aside. In small bowl, stir together apricots and water; cover. Let stand 5 minutes; drain. Meanwhile, in large bowl, beat margarine, granulated sugar, brown sugar and vanilla until well blended. Stir together 1 cup flour, baking soda and salt; gradually add to margarine mixture, beating until well blended. Stir in remaining 1⅓ cups white chips; press mixture onto bottom of ungreased 8-inch square baking pan. Spread softened apricots over cookie base. Stir together wheat germ, remaining 2 tablespoons flour, honey and egg white until blended; crumble over apricots.

3. Bake 30 minutes or until wheat germ is lightly browned. Cool completely in pan on wire rack.

4. In small microwave-safe bowl, stir together reserved white chips and shortening. Microwave at HIGH (100%) 30 seconds; stir. If necessary, microwave at HIGH an additional 15 seconds at a time, stirring after each heating, just until chips are melted when stirred. Using tines of fork, drizzle mixture over top; let stand until glaze is firm. Cut into bars.   *About 16 bars*

HERSHEY'S 50% REDUCED FAT CHOCOLATEY CHIP COOKIES

2¼ cups all-purpose flour
1 teaspoon baking soda
½ teaspoon salt
½ cup (1 stick) 56-60% vegetable oil spread
¾ cup granulated sugar
¾ cup packed light brown sugar

1 teaspoon vanilla extract
2 eggs
2 cups (12-ounce package) HERSHEY'S Reduced Fat Semi-Sweet Baking Chips

1. Heat oven to 375°F.

2. Stir together flour, baking soda and salt. In large bowl, beat spread, granulated sugar, brown sugar and vanilla with electric mixer until creamy. Add eggs; beat well. Gradually add flour mixture, beating well. Stir in chips. Drop by rounded teaspoons onto ungreased cookie sheet.

3. Bake 8 to 10 minutes or until lightly browned. Cool slightly; remove from cookie sheet to wire rack. *5 dozen cookies*

NOTE: To make softer, chewier cookies, add 1 or 2 tablespoons unsweetened applesauce to egg mixture.

PAN RECIPE: Spray 15½ × 10½ × 1-inch jelly-roll pan with vegetable cooking spray; spread batter into pan. Bake at 375°F 18 to 20 minutes or until lightly browned. Cool completely. Cut into bars. *60 bars*

CHOCOLATE CHOCOLATEY CHIP COOKIES: Add ⅓ cup HERSHEY'S Cocoa to flour mixture; follow directions above for mixing and baking.

NUTRITIONAL INFORMATION PER SERVING: 1 Cookie
70 Calories (20 Calories from Fat), 2.5 g Total Fat‡ (4% Daily Value), 1.5 g Saturated Fat (8% Daily Value), 5 mg Cholesterol (2% Daily Value), 60 mg Sodium (3% Daily Value), 13 g Total Carbohydrate (4% Daily Value), <1 g Dietary Fiber (3% Daily Value), 9 g Sugars, 1 g Protein, 0% Daily Value Vitamin A, 0% Daily Value Vitamin C, 0% Daily Value Calcium, 0% Daily Value Iron.

‡ Contains 1 g of Salatrim per serving, only 55% of which is used by the body. Therefore this recipe provides 2 g of available total fat per serving vs. 4.5 g in the HERSHEY'S CLASSIC CHOCOLATE CHIP COOKIES recipe.

PEANUT BUTTER CHIP ORANGE COOKIES

½ cup (1 stick) butter or margarine, softened
½ cup shortening
¾ cup granulated sugar
¾ cup packed light brown sugar
2 eggs
1 tablespoon freshly grated orange peel

1 teaspoon vanilla extract
2¼ cups all-purpose flour
1 teaspoon baking soda
1 teaspoon salt
¼ cup orange juice
1⅔ cups (10-ounce package) REESE'S Peanut Butter Chips

1. Heat oven to 350°F.

2. In large bowl, beat butter, shortening, granulated sugar and brown sugar until light and fluffy. Add eggs, orange peel and vanilla; beat until blended. Stir together flour, baking soda and salt; add alternately with orange juice to butter mixture, beating until well blended. Stir in peanut butter chips. Drop by teaspoons onto ungreased cookie sheet.

3. Bake 8 to 10 minutes or until lightly browned. Cool slightly; remove from cookie sheet to wire rack. Cool completely.   *About 6 dozen cookies*

 TIP

Cool cookie sheets completely before putting more cookie dough on them. Dropping cookie dough on warm cookie sheets causes excess spread.

Peanut Butter Chip Orange Cookies

THREE GREAT TASTES BLOND BROWNIES

2 cups packed light brown
   sugar
1 cup (2 sticks) butter or
   margarine, melted
2 eggs
2 teaspoons vanilla extract
2 cups all-purpose flour
1 teaspoon salt
⅔ cup (of each) HERSHEY'S
   Semi-Sweet Chocolate
   Chips, REESE'S Peanut
Butter Chips, and
HERSHEY'S Premier
White Chips
CHOCOLATE CHIP
DRIZZLE (recipe
follows)

1. Heat oven to 350°F. Grease 15½ × 10½ × 1-inch jelly-roll pan.

2. In large bowl, stir together brown sugar and butter; beat in eggs and vanilla until smooth. Add flour and salt, beating just until blended; stir in chocolate, peanut butter and white chips. Spread batter into prepared pan.

3. Bake 25 to 30 minutes or until wooden pick inserted in center comes out clean. Cool completely in pan on wire rack. Cut into bars. With tines of fork, drizzle CHOCOLATE CHIP DRIZZLE randomly over bars. *About 72 bars*

CHOCOLATE CHIP DRIZZLE: In small microwave-safe bowl, place ¼ cup HERSHEY'S Semi-Sweet Chocolate Chips and ¼ teaspoon shortening (do not use butter, margarine or oil). Microwave at HIGH (100%) 30 seconds to 1 minute; stir until chips are melted and mixture is smooth.

Three Great Tastes Blond Brownies

PINEAPPLE AND WHITE CHIP DROPS

1 cup (2 sticks) butter or
  margarine, softened
1 cup sugar
2 eggs
½ teaspoon vanilla extract
1 can (8 ounces) crushed
  pineapple, with juice
3½ cups all-purpose flour
1 teaspoon baking soda

¾ teaspoon ground
  cinnamon
½ teaspoon salt
¼ teaspoon ground nutmeg
1 cup chopped pecans
1⅔ cups (10-ounce
  package) HERSHEY'S
  Premier White Chips

1. Heat oven to 350°F. Lightly grease cookie sheet.

2. In large bowl, beat butter and sugar until well blended. Add eggs and vanilla; blend well. Blend in pineapple and juice. Stir together flour, baking soda, cinnamon, salt and nutmeg; gradually add to butter mixture, beating until well blended. Stir in pecans and white chips. Drop by tablespoons onto prepared cookie sheet.

3. Bake 10 to 12 minutes or until lightly browned around edges. Remove from cookie sheet to wire rack. Cool completely.   *About 5 dozen cookies*

MINI KISSES BUTTER PECAN SQUARES

½ cup (1 stick) butter,
  softened
½ cup packed light brown
  sugar
1 egg
1 teaspoon vanilla extract
¾ cup all-purpose flour

1¾ cups (10-ounce
  package) HERSHEY'S
  MINI KISSES
  Chocolate, divided
¾ cup coarsely chopped
  pecans, divided

1. Heat oven to 350°F. Grease 8-inch square baking pan.

2. In small bowl, beat butter, brown sugar, egg and vanilla; blend in flour. Stir in ¾ cup MINI KISSES Chocolate and ¼ cup pecans; spread evenly into prepared pan.

3. Bake 25 to 30 minutes or until lightly browned; remove from oven. Immediately sprinkle remaining 1 cup MINI KISSES Chocolate over top. Let stand 5 minutes or until chocolate softens; with knife, spread evenly. Immediately sprinkle remaining ½ cup pecans over top; press gently. Cool completely in pan on wire rack. Cut into squares.　　*About 16 squares*

TOFFEE CRUNCH BLONDIES

2¼ cups all-purpose flour
1 teaspoon baking powder
½ teaspoon baking soda
½ teaspoon salt
½ cup (1 stick) butter or margarine, softened
1 cup packed light brown sugar
2 eggs

2 tablespoons milk
1 teaspoon vanilla extract
1¾ cups (10-ounce package) SKOR English Toffee Baking Bits, divided
1 cup HERSHEY'S Semi-Sweet Chocolate Chips

1. Heat oven to 350°F. Grease 13 × 9 × 2-inch baking pan.

2. Stir together flour, baking powder, baking soda and salt. In large bowl, beat butter and brown sugar until well blended. Add eggs, milk and vanilla; beat well. Gradually add flour mixture, beating well. Stir in 1¼ cups toffee bits and chocolate chips. Spread batter into prepared pan.

3. Bake 30 to 35 minutes or until edges begin to pull away from sides of pan. Remove from oven; immediately sprinkle remaining ½ cup toffee bits over surface. Cool completely in pan on wire rack. Cut into bars.　　*About 36 bars*

COMPANY'S COMING

WHITE CHIP LEMON BARS

1¼ cups all-purpose flour, divided
1 cup granulated sugar, divided
⅓ cup butter, softened
¾ cup HERSHEY'S Premier White Chips

2 eggs, slightly beaten
¼ cup lemon juice
2 teaspoons freshly grated lemon peel
Powdered sugar

1. Heat oven to 350°F.

2. In medium bowl, stir together 1 cup flour and ¼ cup granulated sugar. Cut in butter with pastry blender until mixture resembles coarse crumbs. Press mixture onto bottom of 9-inch square baking pan.

3. Bake 15 minutes or until lightly browned. Remove from oven; sprinkle white chips over crust.

4. In medium bowl, stir together eggs, lemon juice, lemon peel, remaining ¼ cup flour and remaining ¾ cup sugar; carefully pour over chips and crust.

5. Bake 15 minutes or until set. Cool slightly in pan on wire rack; sift with powdered sugar. Cool completely. Cut into bars.   *About 36 bars*

White Chip Lemon Bars

DRIZZLED RASPBERRY CRINKLES

1⅔ cups (10-ounce package) HERSHEY'S Raspberry Chips, divided
1 cup (2 sticks) butter or margarine, softened
1 cup packed light brown sugar
¾ cup granulated sugar

2 eggs
1 teaspoon vanilla extract
2½ cups all-purpose flour
⅓ cup HERSHEY'S Cocoa
1 teaspoon baking powder
1 teaspoon baking soda
1½ teaspoons shortening (do not use butter, margarine or oil)

1. Heat oven to 350°F.

2. Set aside ½ cup raspberry chips. In small microwave-safe bowl, place remaining chips. Microwave at HIGH (100%) 1 minute or until melted when stirred.

3. In large bowl, beat butter, brown sugar and granulated sugar until well blended. Add melted chocolate; beat until well blended. Add eggs and vanilla; blend well. Stir together flour, cocoa, baking powder and baking soda. Gradually beat into chocolate mixture. Drop by rounded teaspoons onto ungreased cookie sheet.

4. Bake 8 to 9 minutes for chewy cookies or 10 to 11 minutes for crisp cookies. Cool slightly. Remove from cookie sheet to wire rack. Cool completely.

5. In small microwave-safe bowl, place reserved chips and shortening. Microwave at HIGH 30 seconds or until chips are melted when stirred. Drizzle over cookies.

About 5 dozen cookies

Drizzled Raspberry Crinkles

FESTIVE FRUITED WHITE CHIP BLONDIES

½ cup (1 stick) butter or
    margarine
1⅔ cups (10-ounce
    package) HERSHEY'S
    Premier White Chips,
    divided
  2 eggs
¼ cup granulated sugar
1¼ cups all-purpose flour

⅓ cup orange juice
¾ cup cranberries,
    chopped
¼ cup chopped dried
    apricots
½ cup coarsely chopped
    nuts
¼ cup packed light brown
    sugar

1. Heat oven to 325°F. Grease and flour 9-inch square baking pan.

2. In medium saucepan, melt butter; stir in 1 cup white chips. In large bowl, beat eggs until foamy. Add granulated sugar; beat until thick and pale yellow in color. Add flour, orange juice and white chip mixture; beat just until combined. Spread one-half of batter, about 1¼ cups, into prepared pan.

3. Bake 15 minutes until edges are lightly browned; remove from oven.

4. Stir cranberries, apricots and remaining ⅔ cup white chips into remaining one-half of batter; spread over top of hot baked mixture. Stir together nuts and brown sugar; sprinkle over top.

5. Bake 25 to 30 minutes or until edges are lightly browned. Cool completely in pan on wire rack. Cut into bars. *About 16 bars*

Festive Fruited White Chip Blondies

PECAN KISS CUPS

½ cup (1 stick) butter or
   margarine, softened
1 package (3 ounces)
   cream cheese, softened
1 cup all-purpose flour
1 egg
⅔ cup packed light brown
   sugar

1 tablespoon butter,
   melted
1 teaspoon vanilla extract
   Dash salt
½ cup coarsely chopped
   pecans
48 HERSHEY'S MINI KISSES
   Chocolate

1. In medium bowl, beat softened butter and cream cheese until blended. Add flour; beat well. Cover; refrigerate about 1 hour or until firm enough to handle.

2. Heat oven to 325°F.

3. In small bowl, stir together egg, brown sugar, melted butter, vanilla and salt until well blended. Shape chilled dough into 24 one-inch balls; place balls into ungreased small muffin cups (1¾ inches in diameter). Press dough evenly against bottom and sides of each cup. Place 2 MINI KISSES Chocolate in each cup. Spoon about 1 teaspoon pecans over chocolate pieces. Fill each cup with egg mixture.

4. Bake 25 minutes or until filling is set. Cool in pan on wire rack. Remove from pan.

About 24 cups

 TIP

For an additional chocolate hit and a neat garnish, lightly press a MINI KISS Chocolate on top of each Pecan Kiss Cup after removing from oven.

ALMOND SHORTBREAD COOKIES WITH RASPBERRY FILLING

¾ cup sliced almonds,
   toasted*
1 cup (2 sticks) butter or
   margarine, softened
¾ cup sugar
3 egg yolks

¾ teaspoon almond extract
2 cups all-purpose flour
RASPBERRY FILLING
   (recipe follows)
Powdered sugar
   (optional)

1. Finely chop almonds.

2. In large bowl, beat butter and sugar until creamy. Add egg yolks and almond extract; beat well. Gradually add flour, beating until well blended. Stir in almonds. Refrigerate dough 1 to 2 hours or until firm enough to handle.

3. Heat oven to 350°F.

4. On well-floured surface, roll about one-fourth of dough to about ⅛-inch thickness (keep remaining dough in refrigerator). Using 2-inch round cookie cutter, cut into equal number of rounds. Place on ungreased cookie sheet.

5. Bake 8 to 10 minutes or until almost set. Cool slightly; remove from cookie sheet to wire rack. Cool completely. Meanwhile, prepare RASPBERRY FILLING. Spread about one measuring teaspoon filling onto bottom of one cookie. Top with second cookie; gently press together. Repeat with remaining cookies. Allow to set about 1 hour. Lightly sift powdered sugar over top of cookies, if desired. Cover; store at room temperature. *About 44 sandwich cookies*

RASPBERRY FILLING: In small saucepan over low heat, combine 1 cup HERSHEY'S Raspberry Chips and ⅓ cup whipping cream. Stir constantly until mixture is smooth. Remove from heat. Cool about 20 minutes or until slightly thickened and spreadable. About 1 cup filling.

*To toast almonds: Heat oven to 350°F. Spread almonds in thin layer in shallow baking pan. Bake 8 to 10 minutes, stirring occasionally, until light golden brown; cool.

TINY MINI KISSES PEANUT BLOSSOMS

½ cup shortening
¾ cup REESE'S Creamy
    Peanut Butter
⅓ cup granulated sugar
⅓ cup packed light brown
    sugar
1 egg
3 tablespoons milk

1 teaspoon vanilla extract
1½ cups all-purpose flour
½ teaspoon baking soda
½ teaspoon salt
Granulated sugar
HERSHEY'S MINI KISSES
    Chocolate

1. Heat oven to 350°F.

2. In large bowl, beat shortening and peanut butter with electric mixer until well mixed. Add ⅓ cup granulated sugar and brown sugar; beat well. Add egg, milk and vanilla; beat until fluffy. Stir together flour, baking soda and salt; gradually add to peanut butter mixture, beating until blended. Shape into ½-inch balls. Roll in granulated sugar; place on ungreased cookie sheet.

3. Bake 5 to 6 minutes or until set. Immediately press MINI KISS Chocolate into center of each cookie. Remove from cookie sheet to wire rack.

About 14 dozen cookies

VARIATION: For larger cookies, shape dough into 1-inch balls. Roll in granulated sugar. Place on ungreased cookie sheet. Bake 10 minutes or until set. Immediately place 3 MINI KISSES Chocolate in center of each cookie, pressing down slightly. Remove from cookie sheet to wire rack. Cool completely.

About 4 dozen cookies

Tiny Mini Kisses Peanut Blossoms

CHOCOLATE FLORENTINES

¼ cup CANDIED ORANGE
    PEEL (recipe on
    page 86)
½ cup (1 stick) butter (no
    substitutes)
⅔ cup sugar
  2 tablespoons milk

2 tablespoons light corn
    syrup
⅓ cup all-purpose flour
1 cup sliced almonds
1 teaspoon vanilla extract
CHOCOLATE FILLING
    (recipe on page 86)

1. Prepare CANDIED ORANGE PEEL.

2. Heat oven to 350°F. Line cookie sheets with heavy duty foil; smooth out wrinkles.

3. In medium saucepan, place butter, sugar, milk and corn syrup. Cook over medium heat, stirring constantly, until mixture boils. Continue cooking, without stirring, until syrup reaches 230°F on candy thermometer or until syrup spins 2-inch thread when dropped from fork or spoon. Remove from heat. Stir in flour, candied orange peel, almonds and vanilla. (To keep mixture from hardening, immediately place pan over hot water.) Drop mixture by level teaspoons onto prepared cookie sheets, placing at least 4 inches apart. (Cookies will spread a great deal during baking.)

4. Bake 8 to 11 minutes or until cookies are bubbly all over and are light brown caramel color. Remove from oven; cool. (Carefully slide foil off cookie sheet to reuse cookie sheet; prepare with foil for next use.) Cool cookies completely on foil; gently peel off foil.

5. Prepare CHOCOLATE FILLING; spread thin layer on flat side of one cookie; gently press on another cookie, flat sides together. Wrap individually in plastic wrap. Repeat with remaining cookies and filling. Store tightly covered in refrigerator. *About 1½ dozen filled cookies*

continued on page 86

Chocolate Florentines

Chocolate Florentines, continued

CANDIED ORANGE PEEL: Cut outer peel (no white membrane) of 2 small navel oranges into ½ inch wide strips. Cut across strips to make ½ ✕ ⅛-inch pieces. In small saucepan, place peel, ¼ cup sugar and ½ cup water. Cook over very low heat until bottom of pan is covered only with glazed peel; do not caramelize. Remove from heat; spoon onto wax paper. Cool.

CHOCOLATE FILLING: In small microwave-safe bowl, place 1 cup HERSHEY'S Semi-Sweet Chocolate Chips. Microwave at HIGH (100%) 1 minute; stir. If necessary, microwave at HIGH an additional 15 seconds at a time, stirring after each heating, just until chips are melted when stirred.

WALNUT MINICHIP BISCOTTI

½ cup (1 stick) butter or margarine, softened	1 teaspoon baking powder
1 cup sugar	¼ teaspoon salt
2 eggs	1 cup HERSHEY'S
½ teaspoon vanilla extract	MINICHIPS Semi-Sweet
½ teaspoon walnut extract	Chocolate
2½ cups all-purpose flour	1 cup ground walnuts

1. Heat oven to 350°F.

2. In large bowl, beat butter and sugar until well blended. Add eggs, vanilla and walnut extract; beat until smooth. Stir together flour, baking powder and salt; gradually add to butter mixture, beating until smooth. (Dough will be thick.) Using wooden spoon, work small chocolate chips and walnuts into dough. Divide dough into four equal parts. Shape each part into a log about 9 inches long. Place on ungreased cookie sheet, at least 2 inches apart.

3. Bake 25 minutes or until logs are set. Remove from oven; let cool on cookie sheet 15 minutes. Using serrated knife and sawing motion, cut logs diagonally into ½-inch slices. Discard end pieces. Arrange slices, cut sides down and close together on cookie sheet.

4. Bake 5 to 6 minutes. Turn each slice over; bake an additional 5 to 6 minutes. Remove from oven; cool on cookie sheets. *About 4 dozen biscotti*

REESE'S NUT BRITTLE COOKIE BARS

1⅔ cups all-purpose flour
2 tablespoons sugar
¾ teaspoon baking powder
½ cup (1 stick) cold butter
    (no substitutes)
1 egg, slightly beaten
2 tablespoons evaporated
    milk

1⅔ cups (10-ounce
    package) REESE'S
    Peanut Butter Chips,
    divided
NUT FILLING (recipe
    follows)

1. Heat oven to 375°F.

2. In medium bowl, stir together flour, sugar and baking powder. Cut in butter with pastry blender until mixture forms coarse crumbs. Stir in egg and evaporated milk; mix until mixture holds together. Press evenly onto bottom and up sides of 15½ × 10½ × 1-inch ungreased jelly-roll pan.

3. Bake 8 to 10 minutes or until golden; cool in pan on wire rack. Sprinkle 1 cup peanut butter chips over crust. Prepare NUT FILLING; carefully spoon over baked crust and chips. (Do not spread; mixture will spread during baking.)

4. Bake 12 to 15 minutes or until filling is caramel colored. Remove from oven; sprinkle remaining ⅔ cup peanut butter chips over top. Cool completely in pan on wire rack; cut into bars.

About 48 bars

NUT FILLING

1½ cups sugar
½ cup (1 stick) butter (no
    substitutes)

½ cup evaporated milk
½ cup light corn syrup
1½ cups sliced almonds

1. In 3-quart saucepan, combine sugar, butter, evaporated milk and corn syrup. Cook over medium heat, stirring constantly, until mixture boils. Stir in almonds. Continue cooking and stirring over medium heat until mixture reaches 240°F on a candy thermometer or until small amount of mixture, when dropped into very cold water, forms a soft ball which flattens when removed from water. (Bulb of candy thermometer should not rest on bottom of saucepan.) Remove from heat; use immediately.

CHOCOLATE CHIPS AND RASPBERRY BARS

1½ cups all-purpose flour
½ cup sugar
½ teaspoon baking powder
½ teaspoon salt
½ cup (1 stick) butter or
  margarine, softened

1 egg, beaten
¼ cup milk
¼ teaspoon vanilla extract
¾ cup raspberry preserves
1 cup HERSHEY'S Semi-
  Sweet Chocolate Chips

1. Heat oven to 400°F. Grease 13 × 9 × 2-inch baking pan.

2. In large bowl, stir together flour, sugar, baking powder and salt. Cut in butter with pastry blender until mixture resembles coarse crumbs. Add egg, milk and vanilla; beat on medium speed of electric mixer until well blended.

3. Reserve ½ cup mixture for topping. Spread remaining mixture onto bottom of prepared pan (this will be a very thin layer). Spread preserves evenly over dough; sprinkle chocolate chips over top. Drop reserved dough by ½ teaspoons over chips.

4. Bake 25 minutes or until golden. Cool completely in pan on wire rack. Cut into bars.

About 32 bars

 TIP

Rich, buttery bar cookies and brownies freeze extremely well. Freeze in airtight containers or freezer bags for up to three months. Thaw at room temperature.

Chocolate Chips and Raspberry Bars

PEANUT BUTTER CHIP TASSIES

1 package (3 ounces)
  cream cheese, softened
½ cup (1 stick) butter,
  softened
1 cup all-purpose flour
1 egg, slightly beaten
½ cup sugar
2 tablespoons butter,
  melted

¼ teaspoon lemon juice
¼ teaspoon vanilla extract
1 cup REESE'S Peanut
  Butter Chips, chopped*
6 red candied cherries,
  quartered (optional)

1. In medium bowl, beat cream cheese and ½ cup butter; stir in flour. Cover; refrigerate about one hour or until dough is firm. Shape into 24 one-inch balls; place each ball into ungreased, small muffin cups (1¾ inches in diameter). Press dough evenly against bottom and sides of each cup.

2. Heat oven to 350°F.

3. In medium bowl, combine egg, sugar, melted butter, lemon juice and vanilla; stir until smooth. Add chopped peanut butter chips. Fill muffin cups ¾ full with mixture.

4. Bake 20 to 25 minutes or until filling is set and lightly browned. Cool completely; remove from pan to wire rack. Garnish with candied cherries, if desired.   *About 2 dozen*

Do not chop peanut butter chips in food processor or blender.

Peanut Butter Chip Tassies

RECIPE INDEX

Almond Joy Bits Sugar Cookies, 60

Almond Shortbread Cookies with Raspberry Filling, 81

Brownies & Bars

Brownie Caramel Pecan Bars, 8

Brownies with Peanut Butter Chips, 42

Butterscotch Blondies, 44

Chewy Rocky Road Bars, 41

Chippy Chewy Bars, 18

Chocolate Chips and Raspberry Bars, 88

Double Chocolate Brownie Bars, 28

Easy Bake Shoppe Marbled Brownies, 46

Festive Fruited White Chip Blondies, 78

Five Layer Bars, 22

Fudgey Raspberry Brownies, 61

Hershey's Chocolate Mint Brownies, 17

Layered Apricot Snacking Bars, 66

Mini Kisses Butter Pecan Squares, 72

Mini Kisses Praline Bars, 56

Oatmeal Toffee Bars, 58

P.B. Chips Brownie Cups, 36

Peanut Butter Cheesecake Brownie Bars, 54

Peanut Butter Chip-Granola Bars, 11

Peanut Butter Chips and Jelly Bars, 30

Reese's Bits Blondies, 32

Reese's Nut Brittle Cookie Bars, 87

Rich Chocolate Chip Toffee Bars, 52

Three Great Tastes Blond Brownies, 70

Toffee Crunch Blondies, 73

Ultimate Chocolate Brownies, 10

White Chip Lemon Bars, 74

Brownies with Peanut Butter Chips, 42

Butterscotch Blondies, 44

Chewy Rocky Road Bars, 41

Chippy Chewy Bars, 18

Chocolate Chip 'n Oatmeal Cookies, 24

Chocolate Chips and Raspberry Bars, 88

Chocolate Florentines, 84

Chocolate Peanut Butter Thumbprints, 40

Cocoa-Chip Cookies, 16

Double Chocolate Brownie Bars, 28

Drizzled Raspberry Crinkles, 76

Drop Cookies

Almond Joy Bits Sugar Cookies, 60

Chocolate Chip 'n Oatmeal Cookies, 24

Chocolate Florentines, 84

Cocoa-Chip Cookies, 16

Drizzled Raspberry Crinkles, 76

Hershey's Classic Chocolate Chip Cookies, 29

Hershey's Classic Milk Chocolate Chip Cookies, 22

Hershey's 50% Reduced Fat Chocolatey Chip Cookies, 67

Hershey's 50% Reduced Fat Forgotten Chips Cookies, 64

Hershey's 50% Reduced Fat Oatmeal Chip Cookies, 62

Hershey's "Perfectly Chocolate" Chocolate Chip Cookies, 6

Hershey's Soft & Chewy Cookies, 14

Miniature Cookies, 35

Oatmeal Butterscotch Cookies, 20

Peanut Butter Chip Oatmeal Cookies, 23

Peanut Butter Chip Orange Cookies, 68

Peanut Butter Chip Pineapple Drops, 50

Pineapple and White Chip Drops, 72

Reese's Chewy Chocolate Cookies, 16

Soft Banana Chip Cookies, 47

Easy Bake Shoppe Marbled Brownies, 46

Festive Fruited White Chip Blondies, 78

Five Layer Bars, 22

Fudgey Raspberry Brownies, 61

Giant Cookies, 35

Halloween Cookie Pizza, 38

Hershey's Chocolate Mint Brownies, 17

Hershey's Classic Chocolate Chip Cookies, 29
Hershey's Classic Milk Chocolate Chip Cookies, 22
Hershey's 50% Reduced Fat Chocolatey Chip Cookies, 67
Hershey's 50% Reduced Fat Forgotten Chips Cookies, 64
Hershey's 50% Reduced Fat Oatmeal Chip Cookies, 62
Hershey's Milk Chocolate Chip Giant Cookies, 12
Hershey's "Perfectly Chocolate" Chocolate Chip Cookies, 6
Hershey's Soft & Chewy Cookies, 14

Jolly Peanut Butter Gingerbread Cookies, 48

Layered Apricot Snacking Bars, 66

Medium-Size Refrigerator Cookies, 35
Miniature Cookies, 35
Mini Kisses Butter Pecan Squares, 72
Mini Kisses Praline Bars, 56
Molasses Snaps, 24

Oatmeal Butterscotch Cookies, 20
Oatmeal Toffee Bars, 58

P.B. Chips Brownie Cups, 36
Peanut Butter Cheesecake Brownie Bars, 54

Peanut Butter Chip-Granola Bars, 11
Peanut Butter Chip Oatmeal Cookies, 23
Peanut Butter Chip Orange Cookies, 68
Peanut Butter Chip Pineapple Drops, 50
Peanut Butter Chips and Jelly Bars, 30
Peanut Butter Chip Tassies, 90
Peanut Butter Cut-Out Cookies, 26
Pecan Kiss Cups, 80
Pineapple and White Chip Drops, 72

Reese's Bits Blondies, 32
Reese's Chewy Chocolate Cookies, 16
Reese's Nut Brittle Cookie Bars, 87
Rich Chocolate Chip Toffee Bars, 52

Rolled Cookies
Almond Shortbread Cookies with Raspberry Filling, 81
Jolly Peanut Butter Gingerbread Cookies, 48
Peanut Butter Cut-Out Cookies, 26

Shaped Cookies
Chocolate Peanut Butter Thumbprints, 40
Giant Cookies, 35
Halloween Cookie Pizza, 38
Hershey's Milk Chocolate Chip Giant Cookies, 12
Medium-Size Refrigerator Cookies, 35

Molasses Snaps, 24
Peanut Butter Chip Tassies, 90
Pecan Kiss Cups, 80
Sugar Doodles, 34
Three-in-One Chocolate Chip Cookies, 35
Tiny Mini Kisses Peanut Blossoms, 82
Toffee Studded Snickerdoodles, 60
Tropical Gardens Cookies, 55
Walnut MiniChip Biscotti, 86
Soft Banana Chip Cookies, 47
Sugar Doodles, 34

Three Great Tastes Blond Brownies, 70
Three-in-One Chocolate Chip Cookies, 35
Tiny Mini Kisses Peanut Blossoms, 82
Toffee Crunch Blondies, 73
Toffee Studded Snickerdoodles, 60
Tropical Gardens Cookies, 55

Ultimate Chocolate Brownies, 10

Walnut MiniChip Biscotti, 86
White Chip Lemon Bars, 74

PRODUCT INDEX

ALMOND JOY COCONUT & ALMOND BITS
Almond Joy Bits Sugar Cookies, 60
Chocolate Chocolate Cookies, 14
Hershey's Soft & Chewy Cookies, 14

HERSHEY'S BUTTERSCOTCH CHIPS
Butterscotch Blondies, 44
Chewy Rocky Road Bars, 41
Chocolate Chocolate Cookies, 14
Cocoa Sugar Doodles, 34
Hershey's Soft & Chewy Cookies, 14
Oatmeal Butterscotch Cookies, 20
Rainbow Sugar Doodles, 34
Sugar Doodles, 34

HERSHEY'S COCOA
Brownies with Peanut Butter Chips, 42
Chocolate Brownie Frosting, 32
Chocolate Chocolate Cookies, 14
Chocolate Chocolatey Chip Cookies, 67
Chocolate Peanut Butter Thumbprints, 40
Cocoa-Chip Cookies, 16
Cocoa Sugar Doodles, 34
Drizzled Raspberry Crinkles, 76
Five Layer Bars, 22
Hershey's Chocolate Mint Brownies, 17
Hershey's "Perfectly Chocolate" Chocolate Chip Cookies, 6
One-Bowl Buttercream Frosting, 10
P.B. Chips Brownie Cups, 36

Peanut Butter Cheesecake Brownie Bars, 54
"Perfectly Chocolate" Chocolate Chip Cookies, 29
Reese's Chewy Chocolate Cookies, 16
Ultimate Chocolate Brownies, 10

HERSHEY'S MILK CHOCOLATE CHIPS
Chocolate Chocolate Cookies, 14
Hershey's Classic Milk Chocolate Chip Cookies, 22
Hershey's Milk Chocolate Chip Giant Cookies, 12
Hershey's Soft & Chewy Cookies, 14
Soft Banana Chip Cookies, 47

HERSHEY'S MINICHIPS SEMI-SWEET CHOCOLATE
Chippy Chewy Bars, 18
Chocolate Chocolate Cookies, 14
Cocoa-Chip Cookies, 16
Hershey's Soft & Chewy Cookies, 14
MiniChip Granola Bars, 11
Tropical Gardens Cookies, 55
Walnut MiniChip Biscotti, 86

HERSHEY'S MINI KISSES CHOCOLATE
Chocolate Chocolate Cookies, 14
Hershey's Soft & Chewy Cookies, 14
Mini Kisses Butter Pecan Squares, 72

Mini Kisses Praline Bars, 56
Pecan Kiss Cups, 80
Tiny Mini Kisses Peanut Blossoms, 82

HERSHEY'S MINT CHOCOLATE CHIPS
Chocolate Chocolate Cookies, 14
Hershey's Chocolate Mint Brownies, 17
Hershey's Soft & Chewy Cookies, 14
Mint Easy Bake Shoppe Marbled Brownies, 46

HERSHEY'S PREMIER WHITE CHIPS
Chocolate Chocolate Cookies, 14
Festive Fruited White Chip Blondies, 78
Hershey's Soft & Chewy Cookies, 14
Layered Apricot Snacking Bars, 66
Pineapple and White Chip Drops, 72
Three Great Tastes Blond Brownies, 70
White Chip Lemon Bars, 74

HERSHEY'S RASPBERRY CHIPS
Almond Shortbread Cookies with Raspberry Filling, 81
Chocolate Chocolate Cookies, 14
Drizzled Raspberry Crinkles, 76
Fudgey Raspberry Brownies, 61
Hershey's Soft & Chewy Cookies, 14
Raspberry Easy Bake Shoppe Marbled Brownies, 46

HERSHEY'S REDUCED FAT SEMI-SWEET BAKING CHIPS
Chocolate Chocolate Cookies, 14
Chocolate Chocolatey Chip Cookies, 67
Hershey's 50% Reduced Fat Chocolatey Chip Cookies, 67
Hershey's 50% Reduced Fat Forgotten Chips Cookies, 64
Hershey's 50% Reduced Fat Oatmeal Chip Cookies, 62
Hershey's Soft & Chewy Cookies, 14

HERSHEY'S SEMI-SWEET CHOCOLATE CHIPS
Brownie Caramel Pecan Bars, 8
Chewy Rocky Road Bars, 41
Chippy Chewy Bars, 18
Chocolate Chip Drizzle, 70
Chocolate Chip Glaze, 26
Chocolate Chip 'n Oatmeal Cookies, 24
Chocolate Chips and Raspberry Bars, 88
Chocolate Chocolate Cookies, 14
Chocolate Drizzle, 38
Chocolate Florentines, 84
Cocoa Sugar Doodles, 34
Double Chocolate Brownie Bars, 28
Easy Bake Shoppe Marbled Brownies, 46
Five Layer Bars, 22
Giant Cookies, 35
Halloween Cookie Pizza, 38
Hershey's Classic Chocolate Chip Cookies, 29
Hershey's "Perfectly Chocolate" Chocolate Chip Cookies, 6
Hershey's Soft & Chewy Cookies, 14
Ice Cream Sandwiches, 29

Medium-Size Refrigerator Cookies, 35
Miniature Cookies, 35
Peanut Butter Cheesecake Brownie Bars, 54
"Perfectly Chocolate" Chocolate Chip Cookies, 29
Rainbow Sugar Doodles, 34
Rich Chocolate Chip Toffee Bars, 52
Soft Banana Chip Cookies, 47
Sugar Doodles, 34
Three Great Tastes Blond Brownies, 70
Three-in-One Chocolate Chip Cookies, 35
Toffee Crunch Blondies, 73
Ultimate Chocolate Brownies, 10

MOUNDS SWEETENED COCONUT FLAKES
Chewy Rocky Road Bars, 41
Chippy Chewy Bars, 18
Peanut Butter Chip-Granola Bars, 11

REESE'S BITS FOR BAKING
Chocolate Chocolate Cookies, 14
Hershey's Soft & Chewy Cookies, 14
Reese's Bits Blondies, 32

REESE'S PEANUT BUTTER
Reese's Bits Blondies, 32
Tiny Mini Kisses Peanut Blossoms, 82

REESE'S PEANUT BUTTER CHIPS
Brownies with Peanut Butter Chips, 42
Chippy Chewy Bars, 18
Chocolate Chocolate Cookies, 14
Chocolate Peanut Butter Thumbprints, 40

Cocoa Sugar Doodles, 34
Halloween Cookie Pizza, 38
Hershey's Soft & Chewy Cookies, 14
Jolly Peanut Butter Gingerbread Cookies, 48
Molasses Snaps, 24
P.B. Chips Brownie Cups, 36
Peanut Butter Chip Glaze, 28, 42
Peanut Butter Chip-Granola Bars, 11
Peanut Butter Chip Oatmeal Cookies, 23
Peanut Butter Chip Orange Cookies, 68
Peanut Butter Chip Pineapple Drops, 50
Peanut Butter Chips and Jelly Bars, 30
Peanut Butter Chip Tassies, 90
Peanut Butter Cut-Out Cookies, 26
Rainbow Sugar Doodles, 34
Reese's Chewy Chocolate Cookies, 16
Reese's Nut Brittle Cookie Bars, 87
Sugar Doodles, 34
Three Great Tastes Blond Brownies, 70

SKOR ENGLISH TOFFEE BITS
Chocolate Chocolate Cookies, 14
Hershey's Soft & Chewy Cookies, 14
Oatmeal Toffee Bars, 58
Rich Chocolate Chip Toffee Bars, 52
Toffee Crunch Blondies, 73
Toffee Studded Snickerdoodles, 60

METRIC CONVERSION CHART

VOLUME MEASUREMENTS (dry)

⅛ teaspoon = 0.5 mL

¼ teaspoon = 1 mL

½ teaspoon = 2 mL

¾ teaspoon = 4 mL

1 teaspoon = 5 mL

1 tablespoon = 15 mL

2 tablespoons = 30 mL

¼ cup = 60 mL

⅓ cup = 75 mL

½ cup = 125 mL

⅔ cup = 150 mL

¾ cup = 175 mL

1 cup = 250 mL

2 cups = 1 pint = 500 mL

3 cups = 750 mL

4 cups = 1 quart = 1 L

VOLUME MEASUREMENTS (fluid)

1 fluid ounce (2 tablespoons) = 30 mL

4 fluid ounces (½ cup) = 125 mL

8 fluid ounces (1 cup) = 250 mL

12 fluid ounces (1½ cups) = 375 mL

16 fluid ounces (2 cups) = 500 mL

WEIGHTS (mass)

½ ounce = 15 g

1 ounce = 30 g

3 ounces = 90 g

4 ounces = 120 g

8 ounces = 225 g

10 ounces = 285 g

12 ounces = 360 g

16 ounces = 1 pound = 450 g

DIMENSIONS

¹⁄₁₆ inch = 2 mm

⅛ inch = 3 mm

¼ inch = 6 mm

½ inch = 1.5 cm

¾ inch = 2 cm

1 inch = 2.5 cm

OVEN TEMPERATURES

250°F = 120°C

275°F = 140°C

300°F = 150°C

325°F = 160°C

350°F = 180°C

375°F = 190°C

400°F = 200°C

425°F = 220°C

450°F = 230°C

BAKING PAN SIZES

Utensil	Size in Inches/ Quarts	Metric Volume	Size in Centimeters
Baking or Cake Pan (square or rectangular)	8×8×2	2 L	20×20×5
	9×9×2	2.5 L	22×22×5
	12×8×2	3 L	30×20×5
	13×9×2	3.5 L	33×23×5
Loaf Pan	8×4×3	1.5 L	20×10×7
	9×5×3	2 L	23×13×7
Round Layer Cake Pan	8×1½	1.2 L	20×4
	9×1½	1.5 L	23×4
Pie Plate	8×1¼	750 mL	20×3
	9×1¼	1 L	23×3
Baking Dish or Casserole	1 quart	1 L	—
	1½ quart	1.5 L	—
	2 quart	2 L	—